BookTales

Joan Hilyer Phelps

UpstartBooks

Fort Atkinson, Wisconsin

To All My "Mamas!"
Anne R. Hilyer, Virginia "Gee-Gee" West, Nell Dillard Phelps,
Tommye Townsend and Eunice Hilyer.
With examples like these, it's no wonder I love books!

Published by UpstartBooks
W5527 Highway 106
P.O. Box 800
Fort Atkinson, Wisconsin 53538-0800
1-800-448-4887

© Joan Hilyer Phelps, 2004
Cover design by Heidi Green, illustrations by Joan Hilyer Phelps

The paper used in this publication meets the minimum requirements of
American National Standard for Information Sciences —
Permanence of Paper for Printed Library Materials. ANSI/NISO Z39.48-1992.

Contents

Introduction .5

Directions for Making Glove Boards . . .6

Methods of Presentation 8

Instructions for Making
Felt Characters 8

Making Patterns From
Other Sources 8

Directions for Making a Felt Glove 8

General Tips 10

Storytimes

✓Angelina on Stage . . . . .13 EP Hol

Baghead .15

✓Bark, George . . . . .17 E Fie

✓Bear Snores On . . . . .21 EP Wil

Ben's Trumpet 24

✓Blueberries for Sal . . . . .26 EP McC

✓Caps for Sale . . . . .29 EP Slo

✓The Cat in the Hat . . . . .32 E Seu

Circle Dogs 38

✓Click, Clack, Moo:
Cows That Type . . . . .41 EP Cro

✓Cloudy with a Chance
of Meatballs . . . . .44 EP Bar

✓Farmer Duck . . . . .47 EP Wad

✓Five Little Monkeys
Jumping on the Bed . . . . .50 BB Chr

✓Goodnight Moon . . . . .53 E Bro

✓How Do Dinosaurs Say Good Night? .60 EP Yol

Is There Room on the Feather Bed? . .62

✓Joseph Had a Little Overcoat . . . . . .69 EP Tab

✓Lilly's Purple Plastic Purse . . . . .74 EP Hen

✓The Magic Hat . . . . .79 EP Fox

✓Max . . . . .81 EP Gra

Mouse Paint 85

My Crayons Talk 89

✓The Paperboy . . . . .93 EP Pil

Sheep on a Ship . . . . .95 E Sha

✓Silly Sally . . . . .99 BB Woo

Six Hogs on a Scooter 109

✓Snowballs . . . . .112 EP Ehl

✓The Stray Dog . . . . .116 EP Sim

Ten Apples Up On Top 119

✓Trashy Town . . . . .122 EP Zim

The Treasure 124

✓Where the Wild Things Are . . . . .126 EP Sen

✓= MPL has of July 05

Introduction

One morning I was preparing to introduce my storytime topic to a group of children and their caregivers. Included in that group were two preschool classes accompanied by their teachers. One of those preschool groups in particular had been by far the most faithful in attendance to my storytimes. I looked forward to seeing them every week and was horribly disappointed if they weren't there. I can't recall the topic for that specific storytime but as I began the introduction I referred to the first book as "one of my favorites." With that, the children began to giggle. This caught me by surprise since I hadn't knowingly said or done anything to warrant their reaction. Curious, I looked to one of the teachers for an explanation. Her response was, "They think it's funny because you say that about every book you read." I couldn't argue with that! I just hadn't realized I verbalized it that often. The point I'm trying to relay is that to make a storytime experience enjoyable for the children, the presenter must first truly enjoy the books themselves.

In the hope that you and I share some favorites in common, I have attempted to increase the odds by choosing books from among my favorites that are well-known to people familiar with children's literature. Some are award-winning books, some are new and some are classics. Again, all of them are on my list of favorites and hopefully some are on your list as well. Included in each chapter is a citation of the book, an original activity to enhance and support the story and a take-home activity to reinforce the children's experience at storytime. If a book I've included is not one you would choose for yourself, the rhyme, fingerplay and/or craft activity could easily be adapted for use with a similarly themed book of your choice.

Methods of Presentation

In my first book, *FingerTales,* the activities consisted of fingerplays which where presented on puppet gloves or as finger puppets. In this book the activities suggest using flannel boards as well as puppet gloves. Since writing *FingerTales* I have also begun making and using what I call "Glove Boards."

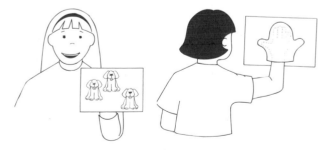

They are simply small flannel boards with a double-thumbed mitten hot glued to the back. (The double thumb allows me to wear it on either hand.) The idea for this arose out of needing larger finger puppets to accommodate larger groups of children. Wearing larger puppets on a glove tends to crowd the puppets—they overlap each other, making it hard to distinguish between them. Wearing the small board on your hand allows the presenter to raise, rotate and maneuver the visual so every child present can see it. It also gives you room to add scenery.

Glove Boards are easy and inexpensive to make so I have them in a variety of colors and sizes! I make them from double thick cardboard, which makes them strong enough that they don't bend but light enough so they don't wear out my arm. I also have made larger boards I can use for flannel board stories. These allow me to move among a group while telling the story. This also helps if some children in the group are having trouble listening to the story—if they can't concentrate from a distance you can take the story closer to them. Another choice for presentation that allows you to move about is a flannel board with an attached strap to wear around your neck. It eliminates the need for an easel and allows you to keep eye contact with your audience. It does, however, take some practice to feel comfortable since you can't see the board as well as you can see a standard flannel board.

Directions for Making Glove Boards

1. Choose the size of board you would like to make and cut two from sturdy cardboard. I recommend a board approximately 10 x 14 inches to start with. After cutting the cardboard, lay it on a piece of felt cut about 1½ to 2 inches larger than the cardboard.

2. Cut the corners of the felt off diagonally, fold the felt over the edges of the cardboard and hot glue in place. Work on sides opposite each other to get a smooth surface, pulling snugly as you go.

3. When finished with the first piece of cardboard, check to see that the corners are covered sufficiently and proceed with covering the second board in the same manner.

4. When both boards are covered, hot glue them together, making sure the unfinished sides of both are facing each other.

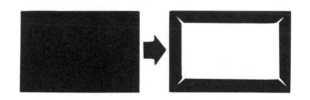

5. Using the pattern provided on page 7, cut out a double-thumbed mitten from matching felt. Determine which side of the board you will use as the front, then hot glue the mitten to the back. Center the mitten on the back, keeping the bottom of the mitten approximately ½ to 1 inch above the edge of the board. The mitten should be a snug fit, which will aid in feeling secure when holding the board. (The felt mitten will "give" a little with use.)

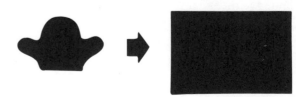

Flannel Board Glove Pattern

Enlarge pattern and extend to desired length.

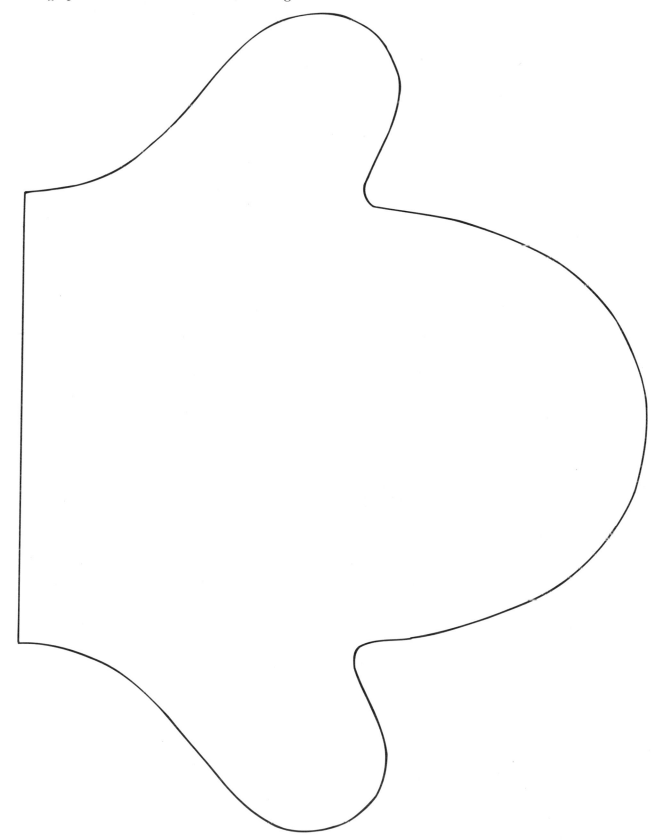

Hints for Using a Glove Board

- Hot glue a clear pocket to the back of your glove board to hold a copy of the fingerplay you are presenting.
- Add a small piece of Velcro to the backs of the characters you use on your Glove Board. (See General Tips on page 10.) This will prevent the characters from dropping off and allow you to stick characters to the back as you remove them.

Methods of Presentation

With the exception of one, I have always made my own flannel boards. They are simple and inexpensive to make and you can customize them to suit your needs. By following the directions for the glove board you can enlarge the size to make a standard board. For variety, use two different colors of felt and make a double-sided board. To make the wearable board, sandwich a strap between the two boards when gluing them together. Make sure to adjust the strap to the proper length for you before you glue it. (The addition of the strap also makes it easy to carry!) Remember not to make the board too wide as it will make it difficult to reach the center. I have also made flannel boards from ornate frames that I've sprayed with gold spray paint. With the addition of black felt, you'll end up with one classy flannel board that's perfect for fairy tales!

Instructions for Making Felt Characters

1. Make photocopies of the patterns and cut them out.

2. Select the appropriate colors of felt. Tape the patterns to the felt, covering them completely. This will keep the patterns from shifting while you cut them out.

3. Use a small hot glue gun to assemble the characters using the illustrations as a guide. Attach Velcro to the back.

4. Finish any details such as eyes, mouths, etc., using a fine-tipped permanent marker. Remember, drawing on felt is different than drawing on paper. It will make cleaner lines if you make a series of connecting dots instead of trying to draw lines.

Making Patterns From Other Sources

There are lots of good sources for characters to use in storytelling that are not in pattern form (pictures for children's books, coloring books, etc.). It's easy to transfer these to pattern forms for characters that have a three-dimensional appearance. I have included examples of two simple drawings and instructions for converting them into patterns. I hope this method works as well for you as it has for me.

1. To make a 3-D pattern I find it is easiest to work with two copies of the picture, one for tracing the individual pieces and the other

for the layout of the pieces somewhat like a puzzle. Begin by visualizing each part as a separate piece.

2. Trace an outline of the main body of the character. This is the middle layer. (The dotted line represents the "hidden" part that can't be seen under the front layer.)

3. Trace all parts in the foreground. These pieces are the front layer.

4. Trace all parts of the back layer. Be sure to include what is not visible for the purpose of attaching them to the opposing layers.

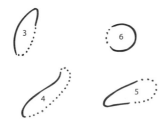

Using the second copy, begin laying the pieces on the corresponding part to align them. Start by placing all of the pieces on the back layer. Secure with a small piece of tape to keep from slipping out of place. Next, place the main body on top of the back layer of pieces. When you're sure they are aligned correctly glue them in place with hot glue. Glue on the front layer and finish by adding final details, such as the eye, with a fine-tipped permanent marker.

The next example is of a person. When I make "people characters" I like to use a double thickness of felt. I think it gives a more lifelike appearance to the character because you can eliminate using ink to add some of the final details. Instead of drawing lines for the fingers you can just make scissor cuts on the lines indicating the fingers. To double the thickness of felt, apply hot glue onto a piece of felt. Use a putty knife or large craft stick to spread the glue, forming a thin, even layer. Apply another piece of felt on top, pressing the two together. (You have to work fairly fast and be very careful while doing this. It's best to work with smaller pieces of felt.) Set aside to cool. This thicker felt makes characters more inflexible, which in turn makes them easier to handle. To assemble the example provided:

1. Use a copy of the drawing to trace all of the parts, visualizing each part as a separate piece. Remember to extend pieces hidden under other parts to allow for gluing. Cut out all of the patterns, tape them to the felt and cut them out. With the arm patterns still taped in place, cut the finger lines to form fingers.

2. To assemble the hair and head, cut out the hair as shown, cutting the solid line that forms the bangs. Slip the head in place under the bangs and glue in place from the back.

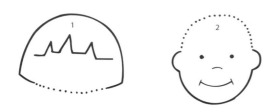

3. Add the neck, remembering that it is the shirt that gives the neck its form.

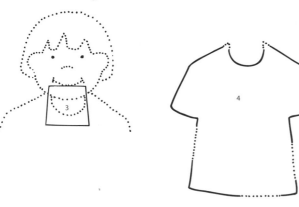

4. Glue the shirt to the neck piece, tucking the very top of the shirt at the neck behind the head and tack in place with glue.

5. Glue the upper arm in place and finish placing and gluing both arms.

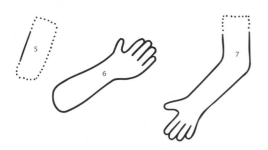

6. Using a fine-tipped permanent marker, add the facial features and you're done!

Directions for Making a Felt Glove

To make a felt glove to use with your finger puppets, use the pattern on page 11 and cut out two gloves. Tape the pattern to the felt to keep it from shifting and extend the length of the pattern to suit your preference. When you have cut out two gloves, stack them on top of each other. Glue them together by working in small lengths to keep the glue from drying too fast. Carefully press the newly glued edge together to ensure a good seal. Wearing gloves during this step is recommended. Apply Velcro to the fingertips of both sides so you may wear it on either hand. You may also wish to use colored Velcro to match your glove. Trim around the glove's edges if necessary. Finish by cutting the glove to length using pinking shears for a finished look.

General Tips

- Always use the sharpest scissors possible.
- Stiff characters are easily maneuvered on the flannel board. Stiffened felt is available at most craft stores. It is perfect for story characters, such as in *Silly Sally*, that are flipped or oddly shaped figures like the round dogs in *Circle Dogs*.
- Use heavy gauged black thread to add details to characters with whiskers like the cat in *The Cat in the Hat*.
- Nothing is more distracting to your presentation than a character falling from the board in the middle of a story! To add a little security, add a small piece of Velcro to the back of each character. Rolls of self-sticking Velcro dots (just the scratchy side) can be found at most school supply stores and are usually sold in rolls of 1,000.
- Although I do recommend using Velcro on the backs of your characters, it sure can give your flannel boards a bad case of the fuzzies! When this happens, use a disposable razor to shave the board. Work in small sections and carefully wipe the blade clean when needed. Finish by rubbing the board with a lint-removing tape roll. It will look brand-new!
- Add details to your characters by using paper punches to make stars, polka dots, hearts, etc., for decorating clothes and hats as in *Five Little Monkeys Jumping on the Bed* and *The Magic Hat*. (Paper punches work especially well on stiffened felt.)

Glove Pattern

Enlarge pattern and extend to desired length.

Angelina on Stage

Written by Katharine Holabird • Illustrated by Helen Craig
Pleasant Company Publications, 2002

Angelina is very excited because she has a part in a grown-up ballet! Not only is she in the ballet, but she has the part of a magic fairy and will actually fly across the stage. Unfortunately, her excitement is short lived when her little cousin Henry also gets a part as an elf. During rehearsals Henry always makes mistakes. Although it bothers Angelina, the grown-ups still adore him (so much so that he is given a line to say as he scampers across the stage). Angelina begins to resent Henry for all the attention he's getting, but on opening night Henry freezes on stage when it's time for him to speak. Will Angelina overcome her jealousy in time to help poor Henry?

Activity: Action Rhyme

After sharing *Angelina on Stage* or any of the delightful Angelina books, lead the children in the following action rhyme.

Spin Around

Sung to the tune: "Are You Sleeping?"
(Suit actions to rhyme.)

Angelina ballerina,
Spin around, spin around.
Put your hands up in the air,
Stretch and keep them way up there.
Now down, down, down,
Touch the ground.

Angelina ballerina,
On your toes, on your toes.
On your toes you're very tall.
Now on your knees, you're very small.
Now sit down,
On the ground.

Take Home: Twirling Ballerina

Materials Needed

- photocopies of ballerina from page 14
- crayons
- tape

Prior to your storytime, photocopy and cut out one ballerina for each child. (Be sure to cut the solid line down to the dotted line between the arms.) Have children color their ballerina. Assist them in folding the bottom on the dotted lines first up and then diagonally to add weight and then folding the arms down in opposite directions. (See illustrations below.) The ballerinas will twirl as they are dropped to the ground.

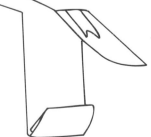

Fold the arms down in opposite directions.

Fold the bottom up.

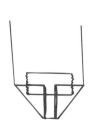

Fold the corners in diagonally.

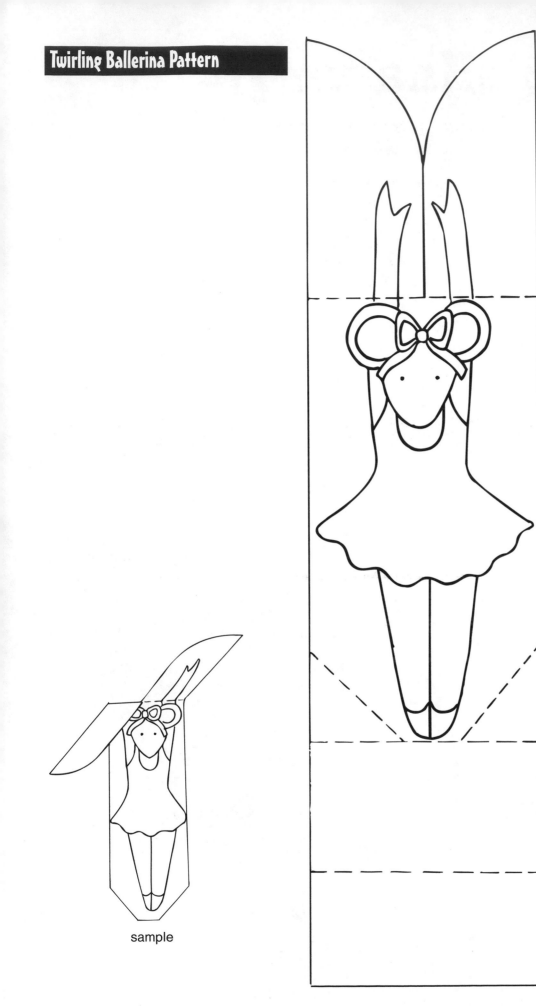

sample

Baghead

Written and illustrated by Jarrett J. Krosoczka
Random House, 2002

One morning, a boy named Josh came down for breakfast wearing a bag on his head. In the bag, he had cut two holes for his eyes and one for his mouth. His mother, bus driver, teacher and soccer coach all question his ability to function while wearing the bag, but Josh continues with his daily activities without removing it. It's not until the whole family is seated around the dinner table that his sister bluntly asks him why he is wearing a bag. That's when he admits he attempted to cut his own hair and removes the bag to show the results! The next morning Josh's sister comes up with the perfect solution to his problem.

Activity: Flannel Board Song

Use the patterns from page 16 to make a boy resembling Josh. Be sure to make the jagged side of the boy's hair as jagged and messy as possible! Also make the bag shape from brown felt and the eyes and mouth holes from black felt. (The bag's edging will be much easier to cut if you use pinking shears!) Prior to your storytime, set up your flannel board by placing the boy on the board and then placing the bag on top of him, covering him completely. (You want the boy to be a surprise during the song.) Set aside the three hole pieces until needed during the song. After sharing *Baghead* with the children, reinforce the delightful story with the following song. (As with the book, be sure to watch the children's faces for those who can relate to Josh's dilemma. Their expressions will be a sure giveaway and not ones to be missed!)

Brown Paper Bag

Sung to the tune: "My Bonnie Lies Over the Ocean"

I once wore a brown paper bag,
(Point to bag on board.)
In which I'd cut three holes, you see.
(Add the two eye holes and mouth.)
I wish I had only cut holes,
And not my own hair. Look at me!
(Remove bag, uncovering boy.)

Don't cut.
Don't cut.
Don't cut whatever you do, you do.
Don't cut.
Don't cut.
Or this might happen to you!
(Point to boy's hair.)

Take Home: Paper Bag Masks

Materials Needed

- medium-size paper bags
- crayons or markers

Prior to your storytime, collect enough paper bags so every child may have one. You will need to have medium-size bags, as lunch bags will be too small. Make a template for the eye and mouth holes so the bags will be uniform in size. Precut all bags. Let the children decorate their bags with crayons and you're done!

Flannel Board Patterns

Enlarge to desired size.

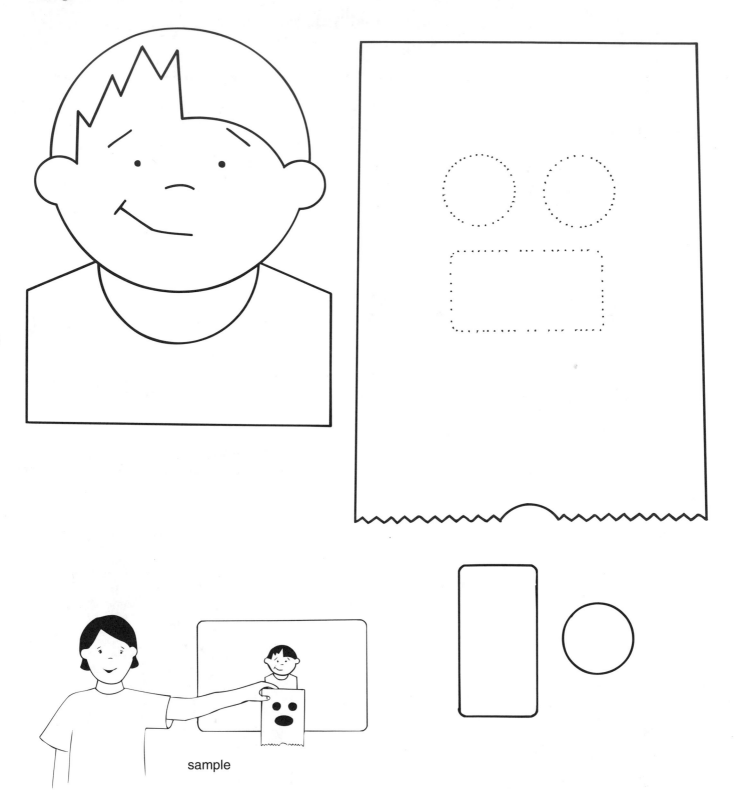

sample

Bark, George

Written and illustrated by Jules Feiffer
HarperCollins, 1999

• — • — • — • — •

George is an adorable puppy, which is why his mother becomes concerned when she asks him to bark and his replies include a meow, a quack, a moo and an oink. She decides to take George to a vet. He solves the problem by reaching deep down George's throat and removing a cat, a duck, a cow and a pig! Needless to say, George's mother is thrilled that the problem is solved. So thrilled that after she kisses the vet and the animals he removed, she decides to show off George on their way home. Unfortunately George's mother is in for another surprise! The illustrations in this book are bold, colorful and delightful—perfect for storytime.

Activity: Flannel Board Song

George

Sung to the tune: "The Wheels on the Bus"

The cat inside of George goes
Meow, meow, meow,
(Place cat on George's tummy.)
Meow, meow, meow,
Meow, meow, meow.
The cat inside of George goes
Meow, meow, meow.
Deep down inside George!

Additional Verses:
Duck / quack, quack, quack
Pig / oink, oink, oink
Cow / moo, moo, moo

Take Home: Puppy Finger Puppet

Materials Needed

- photocopies of puppet from page 20
- crayons
- tape

Prior to your storytime, photocopy and cut out one puppet square per child. After sharing the book and song with the children, hand out the squares and supply crayons so the children can color their puppy. When they are finished, assist them with folding the squares to form the finger puppet as shown in the illustration on page 20.

Enlarge to desired size.

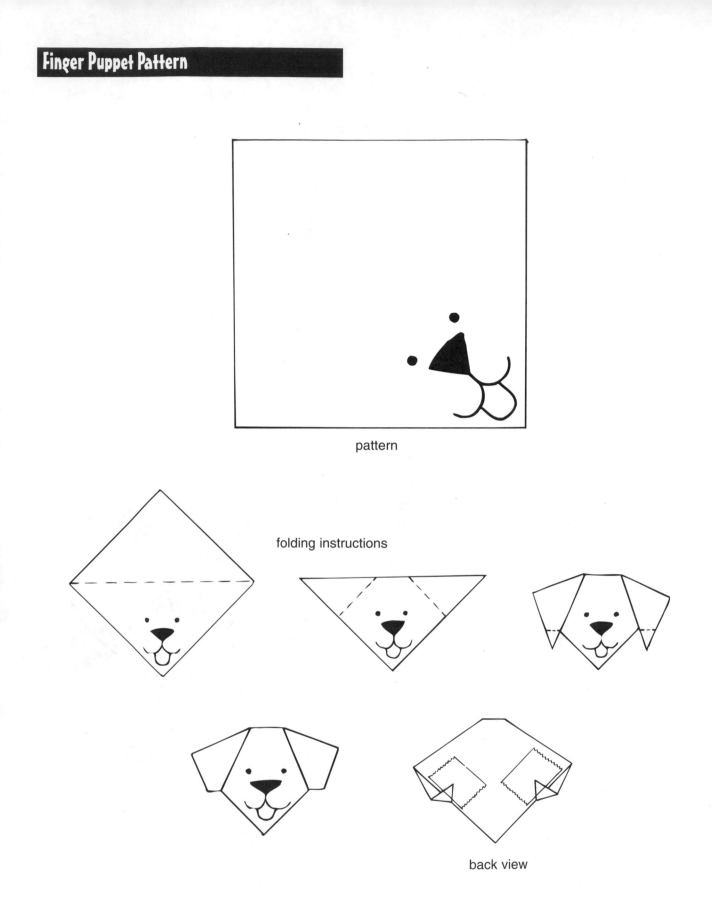

pattern

folding instructions

back view

Bear Snores On

Written by Karma Wilson • Illustrated by Jane Chapman
Simon & Schuster, 2001

As the winter sets in, a big brown bear cuddles up and goes to sleep in his cozy cave. A small mouse happens by and invites himself into Bear's cave seeking temporary shelter from the winter storm. To warm himself up, he starts a small fire, which attracts a rabbit, and together the two fix themselves tea and popcorn while the "bear snores on." One by one, more woodland animals join the party, bringing with them offerings of assorted food. The animals laugh and eat and warm themselves by the fire while the sleeping bear remains oblivious to their presence. Then it happens: while the mouse is seasoning the stew, a small fleck of pepper makes the bear sneeze and the "whole crowd freezes." The bear wakes up grumpy and growling but not for the reasons you would think. The bear is upset because he has missed all of the fun! The animals make it up to the bear by cooking more food and telling more tales until it's the bear who is awake as his new friends snore on.

Activity: Glove Puppet Fingerplay

Using the patterns provided, make five bear puppets from brown felt and a cave Palm Prop from gray and black felt. Finish the details with a fine-tipped permanent marker and hot glue Velcro to the backs for use on a glove. After sharing the delightful "Bear Snores On" with the children, lead them in the following fingerplay.

Five Big and Grumpy Bears

Sung to the tune: "Five Green and Speckled Frogs"

5 (4, 3, 2, 1) big and grumpy bears,
Looking for a cave to share,
Where they can sleep all winter long.
One crossed a mountain wide,
Found a cave and crawled inside.
(Remove one bear from glove.)
Now there are 4 (3, 2, 1, 0) big grumpy bears.

Take Home: Bear Caves

Materials Needed

- photocopies of bears from page 23
- inexpensive paper plates
- crayons
- tape

Prior to your storytime, photocopy and cut out one bear per child. Also prepare one paper plate for each child. Cut out one half of the center of the plate, leaving the rim intact as shown in the illustration on page 23. Next, glue the bear onto the remaining center half of the plate, positioning it as shown in the illustration. Have the children color the bear. Have an example to show and explain that they may want to color underneath the rim because it will be the front of the bear cave when folded. Assist them in folding the rim up to evenly meet the other half and tape together. When completed the bear cave will be three dimensional.

pattern

sample glove puppet

bear pattern

cut on dotted line

sample finished craft

Ben's Trumpet

Written and illustrated by Rachel Isadora
HarperCollins, 1979

— • — • — • — • — • —

A young boy named Ben spends as much time as possible listening to the musicians who play at the Zig Zag Jazz Club in his neighborhood. He enjoys the trombone and the drums but he thinks the trumpeter is the "cat's meow," so much so that he plays an imaginary trumpet everywhere he goes. One day as he is playing his trumpet he hears someone compliment his "horn." When he looks up he sees it's the trumpet player from the club! His happiness is soon shattered, though, when a group of neighborhood children see him pretending to play and tease him about his invisible instrument. Heartbroken, Ben gives up his favorite pastime until the trumpeter questions him about the whereabouts of his horn. When Ben replies that he doesn't have one, the trumpeter takes him to the club and lets him play his! The illustrations are beautiful and capture Ben's emotions and the ambience of the city.

Activity: Action Rhyme

After sharing *Ben's Trumpet* with your group, lead them in this action rhyme in which they can play an imaginary trumpet. Before you begin, demonstrate to the children how to hold their hands and "wiggle" their fingers when playing a trumpet. Use your voice to put emphasis on the action words in the rhyme.

Ben Plays His Trumpet

Sung to the tune: "The Farmer in the Dell"

Ben plays his trumpet high,
(Hold "trumpet" upward, swaying back and forth.)
Ben plays his trumpet high.
Notes float upward to the sky,
Ben plays his trumpet high.

Ben plays his trumpet low,
(Squat and sway trumpet back and forth.)
Ben plays his trumpet low.
Notes go bouncing to and fro,
Ben plays his trumpet low.

Ben plays his trumpet fast,
(Stand and move trumpet quickly back and forth.)

Ben plays his trumpet fast.
Notes come out in a big blast,
Ben plays his trumpet fast.

Ben plays his trumpet slow,
(Move trumpet slowly back and forth.)
Ben plays his trumpet slow.
Notes come out and softly flow,
Ben plays his trumpet slow.

Take Home: Trumpet Necklace

Materials Needed

- tagboard photocopies of trumpet from page 25
- crayons
- yarn

Prior to your storytime, make one photocopy of the trumpet pattern on tagboard for each child and cut out. (Be sure to also cut out the center of the trumpet pattern, indicated by the dotted line.) Provide each child with crayons and a trumpet to color. When they have finished, tie a piece of yarn to the trumpet long enough to make a necklace.

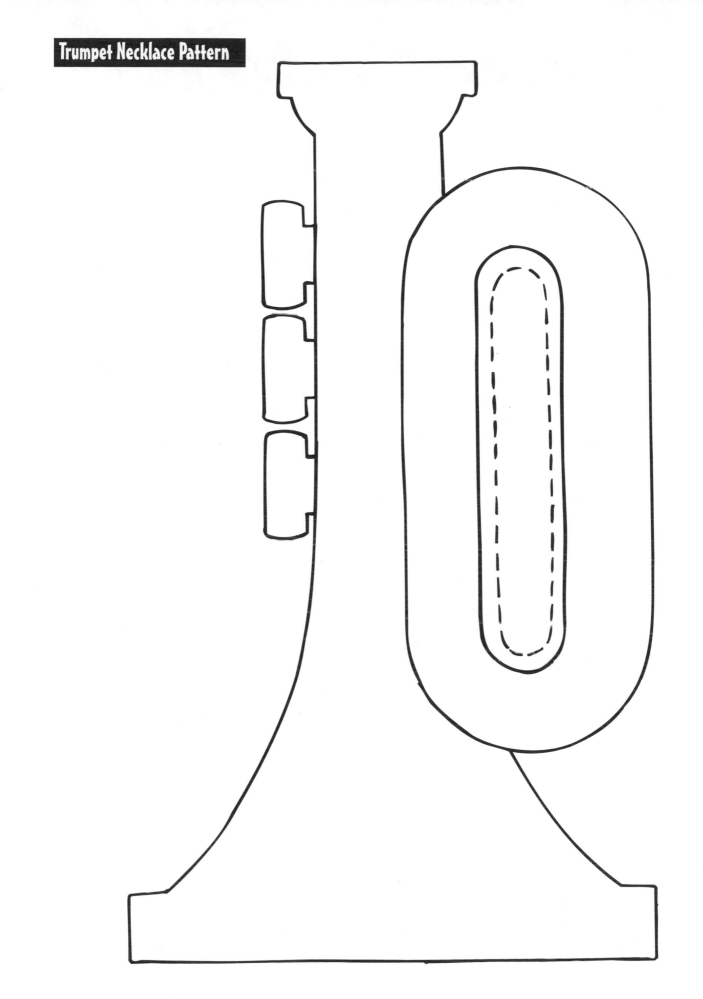

Blueberries for Sal

Written and illustrated by Robert McCloskey • Caldecott Honor Book, 1949
Viking Press, 1948

— • — • — • — • — • —

Little Sal and her mother each take their tin pails and go to Blueberry Hill to pick blueberries for canning. Little Sal picks blueberries and drops them in her pail and listens as they go "kuplink, kuplank, kuplunk." Her mother is a little more serious about her task and as she continues to pick berries, Sal becomes tired and sits in a large clump of bushes to eat the berries around her. As Sal sits eating, Little Bear and his mother make their way up the other side of the hill. Unaware of the other's presence, both mothers are so preoccupied with their berry picking that they don't notice when their children swap places!

Activity: Flannel Board Rhyme

Use the pattern on page 27 to make a pail from gray felt and berries from blue felt. It is up to you to decide how many berries are picked in the rhyme. According to the age of your group, adjust the size of the pail. You may want to enlarge the pattern so that the pail will accommodate more berries if needed. After sharing the book together, lead the children in the following rhyme.

Kerplunk Goes the Berry

Sung to the tune: "Pop Goes the Weasel"

All around the blueberry bush
Goes Sal and Little Bear.
Kerplunk goes the little tin pail,
(Place one berry in top of pail.)
Now one berry is in there!

All around the blueberry bush
Goes Sal and Little Bear.
Kerplunk goes the little tin pail,
(Add one berry.)
Now 2 (3, 4, 5…) berries are in there.

Take Home: Pails

Materials Needed

- photocopies of pail from page 28
- crayons
- pipe cleaners
- tape

Prior to your storytime, photocopy and cut out one pail per child as needed for your group. Punch holes in the pail where indicated. Have children color the pails and attach pipe cleaners for the handles when finished. You may also want to have a supply of blueberries cut from construction paper for the children to add to their pails.

Adjust to desired size.

Pail Pattern

Adjust to desired size.

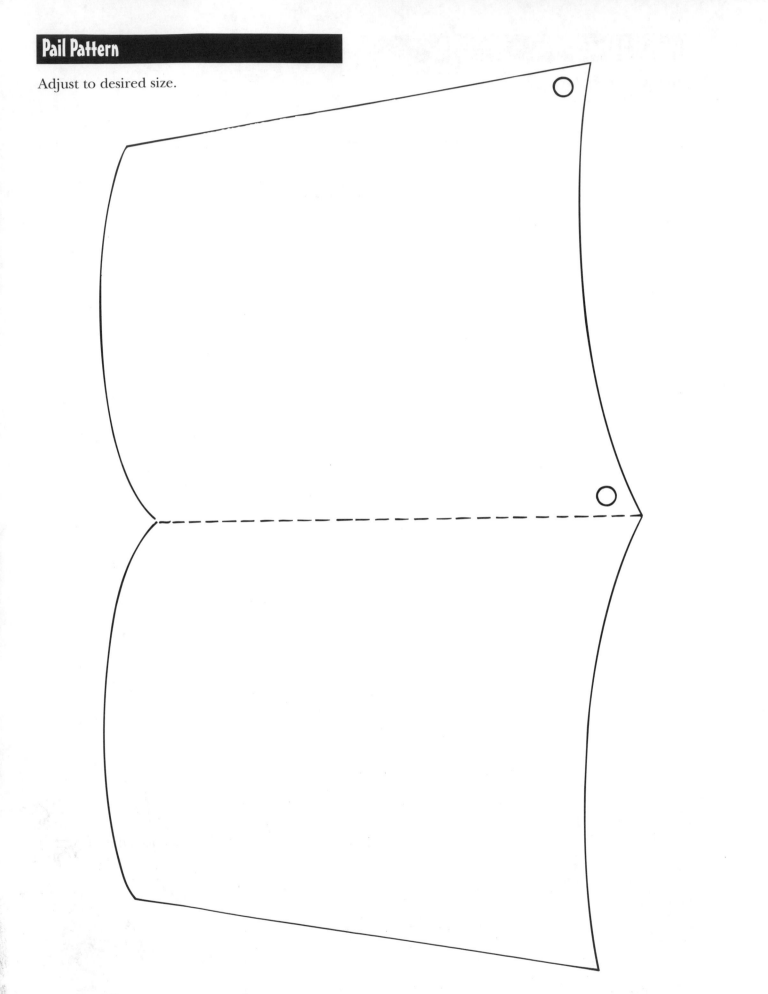

Caps for Sale

Written and illustrated by Esphyr Slobodkina
William R. Scott, Inc., 1940

● ─ ● ─ ● ─ ● ─ ● ─ ●

A peddler selling caps carries his wares in a most unusual way—not on his back like most peddlers, but on his head! He is also very particular about the order in which he carries them, making sure that stacked on top of his own checked cap are a bunch of gray caps, then brown, then blue and red caps at the very top. As he walks carefully through the town he cries, "Caps! Caps for sale! Fifty cents a cap!" One day he has such bad luck with selling the caps that he decides to go for a walk in the country. The walk tires him, so he takes a nap as he sits beneath a tree. While he is sleeping, monkeys in the tree take the hats. The poor peddler wakes to find he has only his own checked cap left! He outwits the monkeys, much to his surprise, after the frustrating encounter, then continues on his rounds calling "Caps! Caps for sale! Fifty cents a cap!" Needless to say, this book is a classic, loved by adults as well as children who never seem to tire of hearing it!

Activity: Flannel Board Rhyme

Caps for Sale lends itself to an endless amount of activities. Most of the ones I am familiar with center on those mischievous monkeys, which is why I decided to highlight the peddler in the following activity.

Use the patterns from page 30 to make the peddler and five caps from the appropriate colors of felt. For the peddler's pants and cap use white felt and then draw lines horizontally and vertically with a fine-tipped permanent marker. As for the five caps, you may want to make them all one color, choosing a color from the caps mentioned in the story (gray, brown, blue and red) or make one from each color. After sharing *Caps for Sale* with your group, lead them in the following rhyme.

The Peddler

Sung to the tune: "Row, Row, Row Your Boat"

A peddler selling 5 (4, 3, 2, 1) new caps,
Stacked neatly on his head,
Sat beneath a tree to nap,
But lost one cap instead!
(Remove one cap from peddler's head.)

Take Home: The Peddler's Caps

Materials Needed

- photocopies of peddler and caps from page 31
- cardboard paper towel tubes with cardboard bases
- gray, brown, blue and red crayons
- glue sticks

Prior to your storytime, photocopy and cut out one peddler with four sets of caps for each child. Also collect a paper towel tube for each child and hot glue a cardboard base to the bottom. Supply each child with the materials. Using a completed craft, demonstrate to the group how to color the hats according to those in the book and glue them to the tube. Depending on their age, the children may be able to use the example to stack the caps in the same order mentioned in the story. (Reread that section of the story to reinforce the sequencing of the colors.)

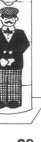

Adjust to desired size.

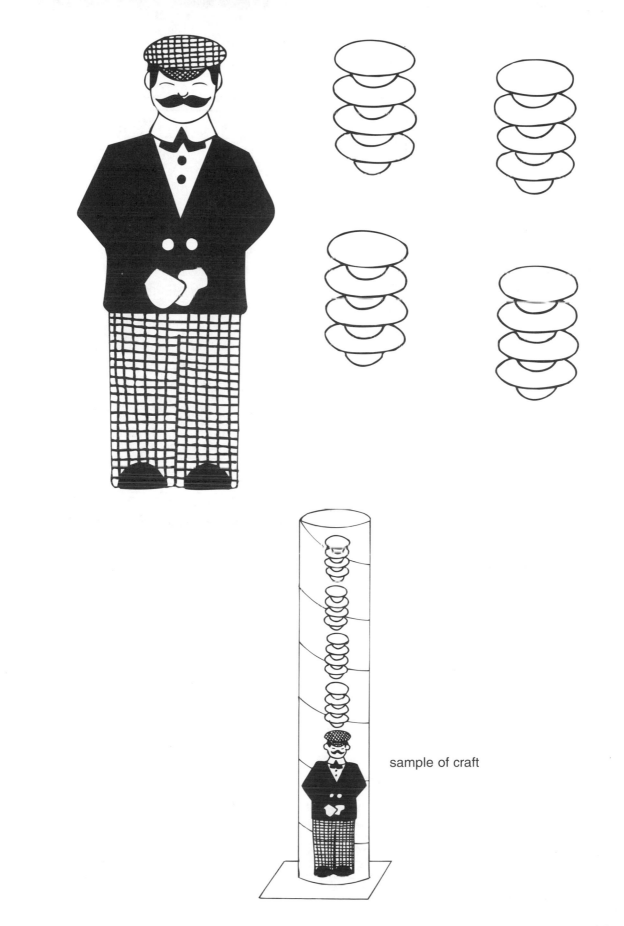

sample of craft

The Cat in the Hat

Written and illustrated by Dr. Seuss
Random House, 1957

This book hardly needs any introduction. It's the classic story of the mischievous cat who comes to visit two bored children on a rainy afternoon while their mother is out. He wreaks havoc in the house with the help of Thing One and Thing Two as the children and their goldfish helplessly stand by. Now that the house is turned upside down and looks beyond repair, how will they ever get it cleaned up before their mother returns?

Activity: Flannel Board Rhyme

Use the patterns from pages 33–35 to make the cat, the umbrella and five goldfish (in their bowls) from the appropriate colors of felt. Included in the patterns are dotted lines to assist in placing the parts together. Before presenting the rhyme, place the cat and his umbrella on the flannel board. Share the book with the children, then lead them in the rhyme.

Up, Up, Up

The Cat in the Hat
Is a talented fellow.
Watch as he balances 1 fish, *(Add one fish.)*
Up on top of an umbrella!

Up-up-up is the name
Of the game and it's true.
Up-up-up goes another, *(Add one fish.)*
Now there are 2!
(Pause before saying number to let children reply.)

"Look at me!" says the Cat,
"Look at me and you'll see."
Up-up-up goes another,
Now there are 3!
(Pause before saying number to let children reply.)

"This is good!" says the Cat,
"But I can do more!"
Up-up-up goes another,
Now there are 4!
(Pause before saying number to let children reply.)

"Now watch us!" says the fish,
"Watch us swim, splash and dive!"
Up-up-up goes another,
Now there are 5!
(Pause before saying the number to let children reply.)

"Very good!" says the Cat,
"Now my trick's almost done,
Now backwards let's count them,
5, 4, 3, 2 and 1."
(Encourage children to help as you point to each fish.)

Take Home: Cat in the Hat Paper Bag Puppet

Materials Needed

- photocopies of puppet from pages 36–37
- crayons or markers
- paper bags (lunch size)
- tape

In preparation for the children's arrival, photocopy and cut out one puppet set per child. To close your storytime, have the children color a puppet. Assist them in taping it to the bag. (The dotted lines near the mouth show where the top should overlap the bottom.)

Adjust to desired size.

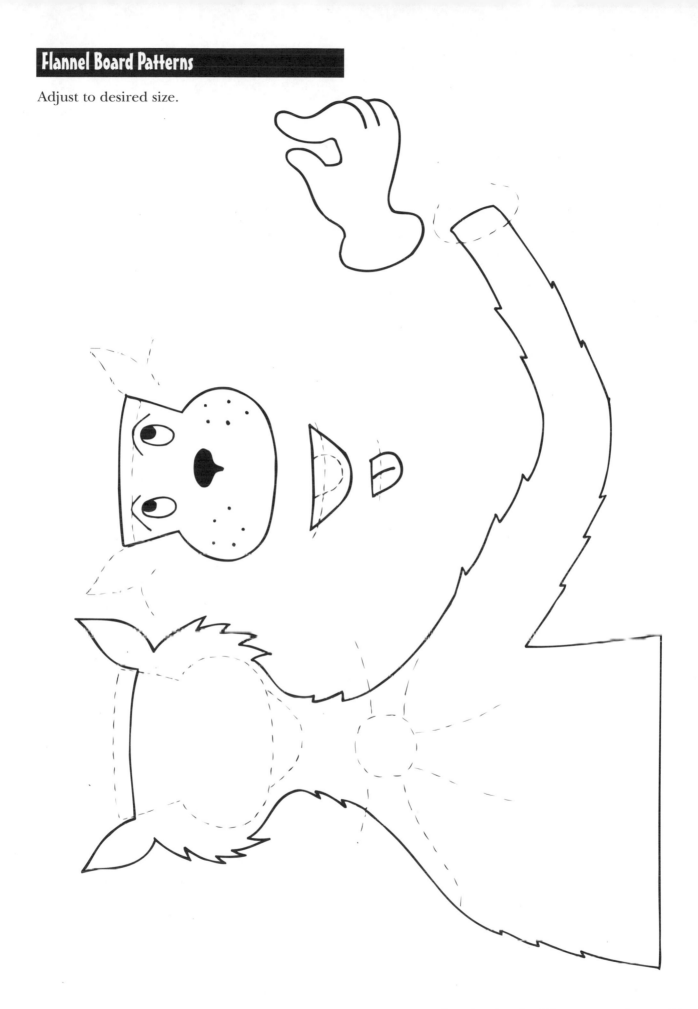

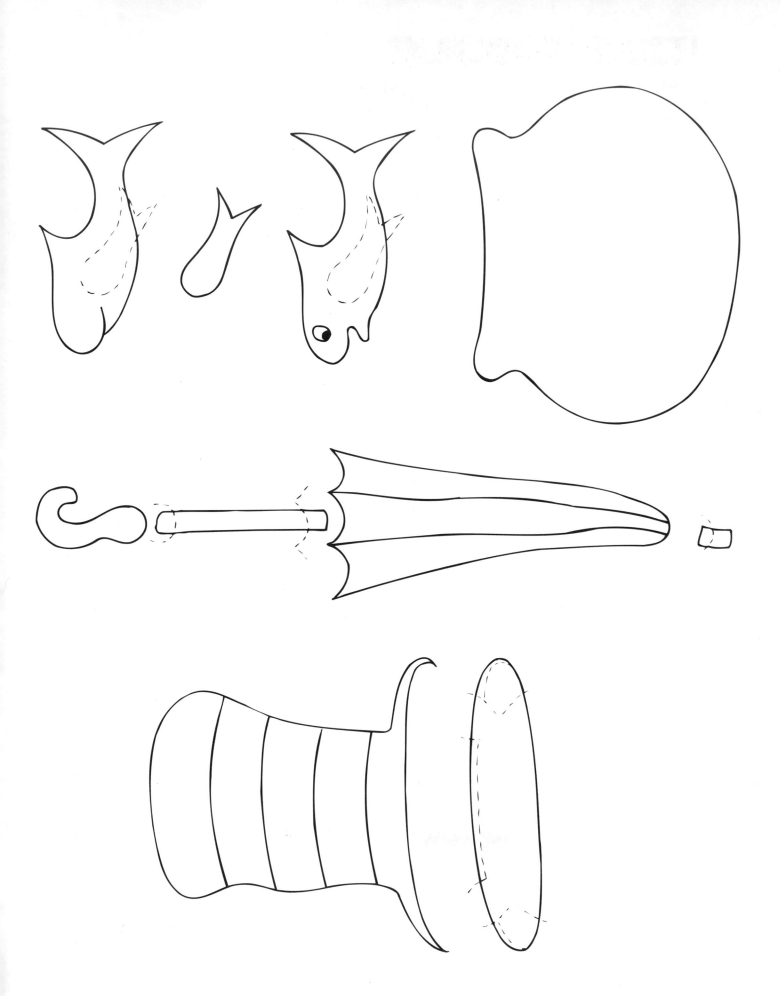

sample of board

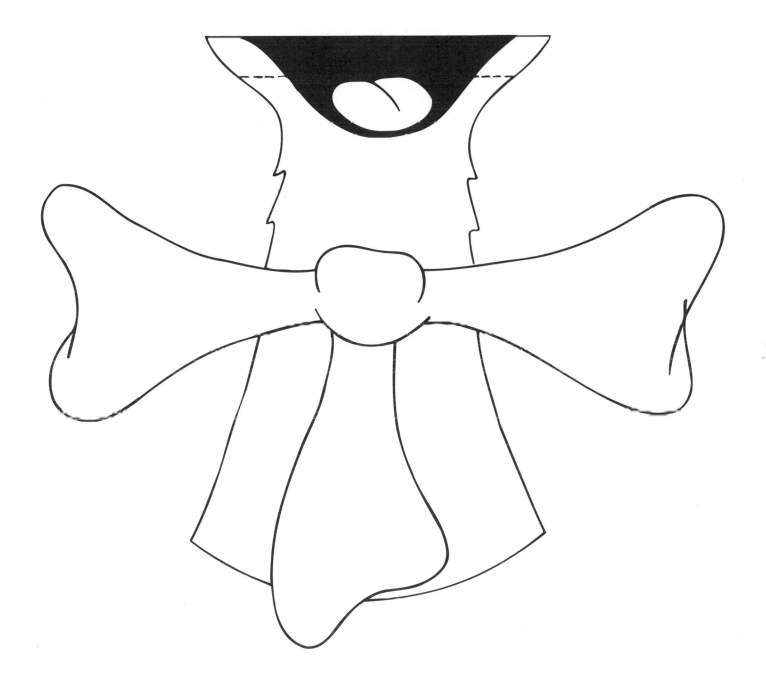

Circle Dogs

Written by Kevin Henkes • Illustrated by Dan Yaccarino
Greenwillow Books, 1998

Experience a day in the life of two dogs! These roundabout dogs are called circle dogs because of their ability to form circles when napping. The circle dogs live with a family in a square house with a square yard where they dig circle holes and eat circle snacks. "Mama calls them pooches, Papa calls them hounds," but mostly they are lots of fun! They couldn't help but be with the combined talents of Kevin Henkes and Dan Yaccarino. This is a delightful book for storytime!

Activity: Flannel Board Rhyme

Use the pattern from page 39 to make five dogs from felt. If you can find stiffened felt at your craft store it would be the best choice for this project as these characters are a little floppy. (The stiffened felt makes positioning and handling oddly shaped characters so much easier!) After sharing *Circle Dogs* with your group, present the following rhyme on the flannel board.

Spin Around

Sung to the tune: "Three Blind Mice"

5 (4, 3, 2, 1) circle dogs,
5 (4, 3, 2, 1) circle dogs,
Chasing their tails,
Chasing their tails.
Around and around and around they sail.
They make a circle by chasing their tails.
One got too dizzy and down he fell!
(Remove one dog from flannel board.)
4 circle dogs.

Take Home: Circle Dog Bracelets

Materials Needed

- tagboard
- photocopies of dog bracelets from page 40
- crayons
- tape

Prior to your storytime, photocopy one bracelet per child onto tagboard. Cut the bracelets out. Let the children color the bracelets. Assist them with forming the dogs into circles around their wrist and taping them together.

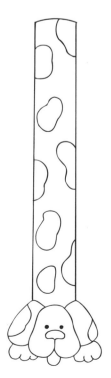

Adjust to desired size.

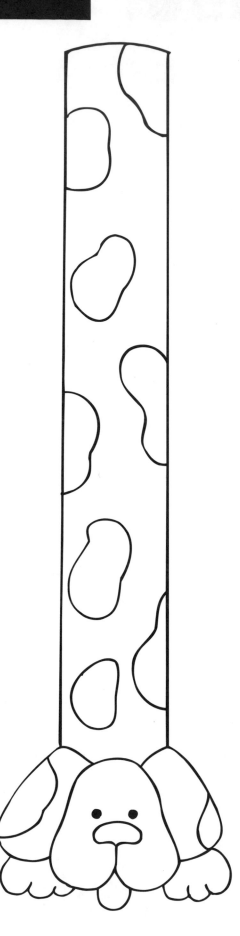

Click, Clack, Moo: Cows That Type

Written by Doreen Cronin • Illustrated by Betsy Lewin
Caldecott Honor Book, 2001 • Simon & Schuster, 2000

━━━━●━━━━●━━━━●━━━━●━━━━●━━━━

After Farmer Brown's cows find an old typewriter in the barn they spend all their time typing. All day long he hears "Click, clack, moo" coming from the barn. And if that isn't bad enough, he finds a typewritten note, addressed to him, requesting electric blankets. When Farmer Brown refuses, the cows go on strike and send him another note by Duck (a neutral party) stating that the chickens are also cold and have joined in their strike. Farmer Brown stands firm and demands his milk and eggs! After an emergency meeting, the cows decide to exchange the typewriter for the blankets and send Duck to deliver the note. The farmer accepts this offer, leaves the blankets outside the barn and waits for Duck to return to him with the typewriter. Will the farmer receive the typewriter or do the ducks have demands of their own? Children absolutely love this book, and who wouldn't? It is loads of fun for all!

Activity: Flannel Board Song

Use the pattern from page 42 to make five cows from felt that resemble the cows in the book. Begin with all five cows on your flannel board. Share *Click, Clack, Moo: Cows That Type*, then lead the group in the following song.

Click, Click, Clack

Sung to the tune: "Five Green and Speckled Frogs"

5 (4, 3, 2, 1) cows type click, click, clack.
Each wants a blanket on its back.
A blanket to keep them nice and warm.
Moo, moo, moo.

Duck takes the note, quack, quack,
The farmer sends one blanket back.
(Remove one cow.)
Now there are 4 (3, 2, 1, 0) cows left to type.

Take Home: Cowbells

Materials Needed

- paper cups
- markers
- pipe cleaners
- "jingle" bells
- yarn

Prior to your storytime, prepare the paper cups by making two holes in the bottom of each cup as shown in the illustration on page 43. Have the children color their cups. Then, demonstrate how to assemble the cowbells. First, thread the bell onto the pipe cleaner, centering the bell in the middle. Next, put both ends of the pipe cleaner through the holes of the cup from the inside. Twist the ends of the pipe cleaner together, forming a loop and securing the bell inside the cup. Thread yarn through the loop, to form a cowbell necklace.

Flannel Board Pattern

Adjust to desired size.

sample of board

Cloudy with a Chance of Meatballs

Written by Judi Barrett • Illustrated by Ron Barrett • Atheneum, 1978

After a pancake flipping incident jars his memory, a grandfather tells his two grandchildren a tall tale about a town named Chewandswallow where there aren't any grocery stores. In fact, the only food available to the townspeople falls from the sky three times a day, at breakfast, lunch and dinnertime. It never rains or snows in Chewandswallow, but they still have weather reports on the local news that forecast the meals expected for the day. All is well in the town, as there is always plenty of food for everyone, until the weather takes an unusual turn and the food that was once delicious becomes unappetizing. Instead of frankfurters and lamb chops there is overcooked broccoli, brussel sprouts with peanut butter and Gorgonzola cheese. There is even a storm of pancakes so large the school is forced to close! The people living in Chewandswallow decide to abandon their town and set sail for new land on boats made of giant pieces of stale bread, never to return. Be prepared for excitement when presenting this book to your group! The illustrations of the adventures of the people in Chewandswallow are very detailed and encourage lots of discussion and remarks from the children.

Activity: Flannel Board Rhyme

Make five meatballs and a cloud to use on your flannel board similar to those in the illustration at right. They can be assembled like small pillows, stuffing them with a little fiberfill, to give them a more meatball-like appearance. (Or adapt the size to use on a fingerplay glove with the cloud as a palm prop.) After sharing *Cloudy With a Chance of Meatballs* with your group, lead them in the following fingerplay.

Five Enormous Meatballs

Sung to the tune: "Row, Row, Row Your Boat"

5 (4, 3, 2, 1) enormous meatballs
In a cloud up high.
Here comes one, *(Remove one meatball.)*
We'd better run!
It's falling from the sky!

sample of board

Take Home: Spaghetti Slurping Man

Materials Needed

- photocopies of man from page 46 on tag-board
- crayons
- white string
- crayons

Prior to your storytime, photocopy and cut out one man and one meatball for each child in your group, making sure to punch a hole beneath his mustache where indicated. Have children color the man and the meatball. Assist them in assembling the parts. First tape the string spaghetti to the back of the meatball. (This can also be done ahead of time with a dab of hot glue to save time with larger groups.) Next thread the other end of the string through the man's mouth and tie it into a loop large enough for the child's finger. (Or tie it to a button or craft stick they could hold that would keep the string from slipping back through the hole.) Demonstrate to the children how to pull the string to make the man slurp his spaghetti as shown in the illustration.

Farmer Duck

Written by Martin Waddell • Illustrated by Helen Oxenbury
Candlewick Press, 1992

● ━━━ ● ━━━ ● ━━━ ● ━━━ ●

A duck who lives with a farmer becomes tired and "weepy" from overwork due to the farmer's laziness. The farmer stays in bed all day as the duck tends to the many chores that accompany life on a farm. The duck brings the sheep from the hill, puts the hens in their house and brings the cow from the field as the farmer calls to him from the bedroom window, "How goes the work?" The duck also does the household chores, including bringing the farmer his meals in bed! The hens, the cow and the sheep love the duck and become concerned for their friend's well-being. They hold a meeting one night, make a plan for the morning and just before dawn they creep into the farmer's house. Quietly, they make their way through the house, up the stairs and under the farmer's bed where they begin to wriggle about, rocking the bed, which wakes the farmer. The farmer is so frightened that he flees with the animals chasing after him and he never returns. When the poor duck awakes to begin his chores the animals return to tell their friend the story. The duck and his friends are so overjoyed that they begin mooing and baaing and quacking and clucking as they set to work on their farm. The full-size illustrations in this book are as beautiful as the story is charming! A perfect storytime book.

Activity: Action Rhyme

After sharing *Farmer Duck* with the children, lead them in this action rhyme in which you and the group can act out the duck's chores as you sing.

Farmer Duck's Chores

Sung to the tune: "So Early in the Morning"

This is the way Duck saws the wood,
Saws the wood, saws the wood.
This is the way Duck saws the wood,
While the farmer stays in bed!

This is the way Duck digs in the garden,
Digs in the garden, digs in the garden.
This is the way Duck digs in the garden,
While the farmer stays in bed!

This is the way Duck scrubs the dishes,
Scrubs the dishes, scrubs the dishes.
This is the way Duck scrubs the dishes,
While the farmer stays in bed!

This is the way Duck irons the clothes,
Irons the clothes, irons the clothes.
This is the way Duck irons the clothes,
While the farmer stays in bed!

This is the way Duck picks the apples,
Picks the apples, picks the apples.
This is the way Duck picks the apples,
While the farmer stays in bed!

Take Home: Quacking Duck

Materials Needed

- clothespins
- photocopies of duck from page 49
- crayons or markers
- glue

Prior to your storytime, photocopy and cut out one duck per child. Collect one clothespin per child for the duck's bill and paint each with either orange or yellow non-toxic spray paint. (You could also have the children color the bill with markers.) During craft time, have children color one duck. Assist them in applying the bill. This can be done with tacky glue, but it will need time to dry. The best no-waiting-required method is with a low-temp glue gun. If your situation allows this to be done safely, there will only be minimum cooling time involved before the children can play with their duck. Either way, remember to glue the duck to only one leg of the clothespin, allowing the other to move freely so it will open and close.

Five Little Monkeys Jumping on the Bed

Retold and illustrated by Eileen Christelow
Clarion Books, 1991

The author has turned the classic fingerplay into a picture book. It begins with the monkeys getting ready for bed. They take a bath, put on their pajamas, brush their teeth and say goodnight to their Mama—then the fun begins! Just like in the fingerplay, one by one they fall from the bed. Mama calls the doctor and the doctor says, "No more monkeys jumping on the bed!" When all her little monkeys are finally asleep in bed, Mama goes to bed herself. But does she go to sleep?

Activity: Fingerplay Rhyme/Song

Use the patterns from page 51 to make five monkeys with bodies of brown felt and faces in a lighter color. Use the clothes patterns to cut out and decorate little felt outfits for the monkeys. You can add designs with fine-tipped permanent markers or use paper punches to make dots, stars, etc. Add Velcro to the backs of the monkeys to use on a puppet glove. After sharing the book, lead the children in the following rhyme.

Jumping Monkeys

Sung to the tune: "Three Blind Mice"

5 (4, 3, 2, 1) little monkeys,
5 (4, 3, 2, 1) little monkeys,
Jumping in a row,
Jumping in a row,
They're jumping fast, they're jumping slow,
(Suit actions to words.)
They're jumping high, they're jumping low.
(Suit actions to words.)
They jumped so much one broke his toe!
(Remove one monkey.)
4 (3, 2, 1, 0) little monkeys.

Take Home: Monkeys

Materials Needed

- photocopies of monkey on tagboard from page 52
- pipe cleaners (three for each child)
- crayons or markers

Prior to your storytime, photocopy and cut out one monkey for each child. Punch holes for the arms and legs where indicated. Have the children color their monkey. Then, demonstrate how to weave the pipe cleaners through the holes to form arms and legs. Secure these into place with the third pipe cleaner that also acts as the tail. (See the diagram on page 52.)

Monkey Fingerplay Patterns

sample monkeys

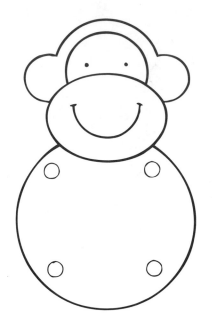

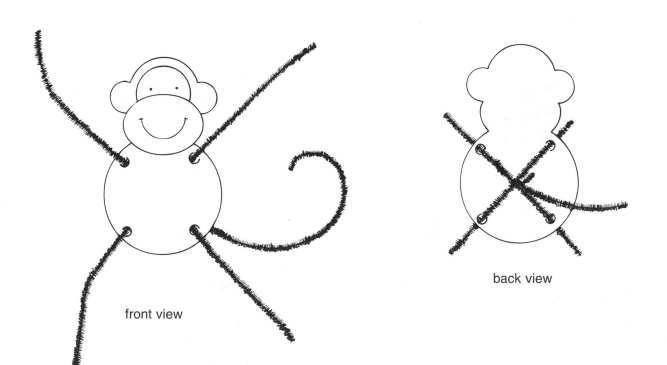

front view

back view

Goodnight Moon

Written by Margaret Wise Brown • Illustrated by Clement Hurd
Scholastic, 1947

■━━ ● ━━■ ● ■ ● ■━━ ● ━━■

In this classic rhyming book a little rabbit is getting ready for bed and saying good-night to different objects in his room. The illustrations include color pictures of the entire room and black-and-white close-ups of the rhyming objects found in the room. As the story progresses, subtle changes in the room can be seen. A little mouse moves from place to place throughout the room. The moon, viewed from the bedroom window, rises in the night sky. The time on the clock progresses along with the story. Hunting for these changes makes this a delightful book for storytime if the group is small enough to share the illustrations up close. The rhyming text invites participation from the children as well.

Activity: Flannel Board Rhyme

Use the patterns from pages 54–58 to make the pairs of rhyming objects found in the book. The patterns are sized so that the second object of each rhyming pair can be hidden beneath the first. In preparation for storytime, set up your flannel board by hiding the kitten under the mitten, the mouse under the house and so on. After sharing *Goodnight Moon* with your group, lead them in the rhyme. Pause before uncovering each hidden object, giving the children time to guess the rhyme. Remind them beforehand that they are the same objects found in the bunny's bedroom.

Say Goodnight

Bedtime is here,
It's time to say goodnight.
Then pull the covers up
And snuggle down tight!

Goodnight mitten,
Goodnight kitten.
(Remove mitten, uncovering the kitten.)

Goodnight house,
Goodnight mouse.
(Remove house, uncovering the mouse.)

Goodnight bear,
Goodnight chair. *(Remove bear.)*

Goodnight clock,
Goodnight sock. *(Remove clock).*

Goodnight balloon,
Goodnight moon! *(Remove balloon.)*

Take Home: Goodnight Doorknob Hanger

Materials Needed

- photocopies of doorknob hanger from page 59 on tagboard
- crayons or markers
- glue
- glitter (silver)

Prior to your storytime, photocopy onto tag-board and cut out enough doorknob hangers to supply each child in your group with one. Be sure to cut out the circle indicated by the dotted line. Have the children color a hanger. When completed let them dab glue on each star and then sprinkle with glitter, tapping the excess off onto paper for reuse.

Adjust to desired size.

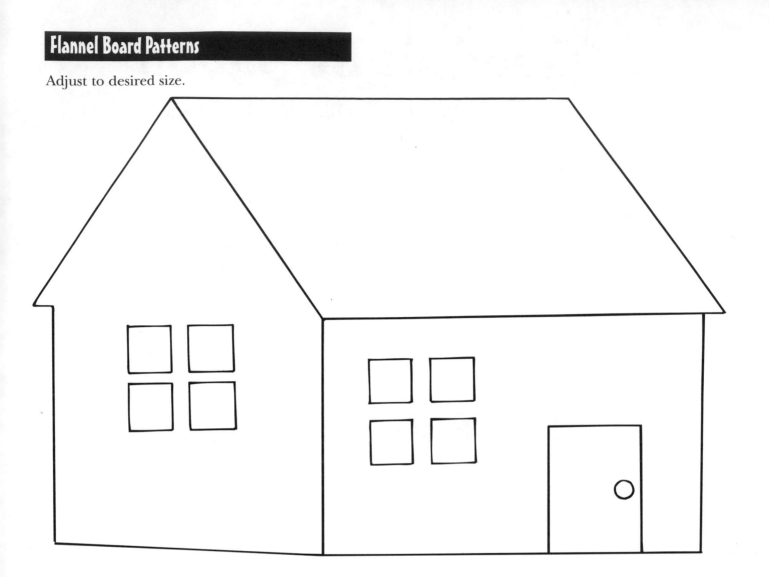

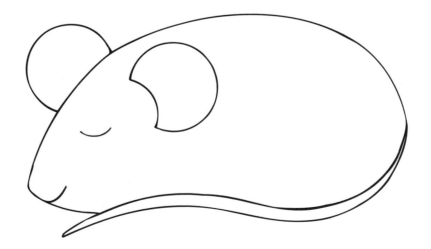

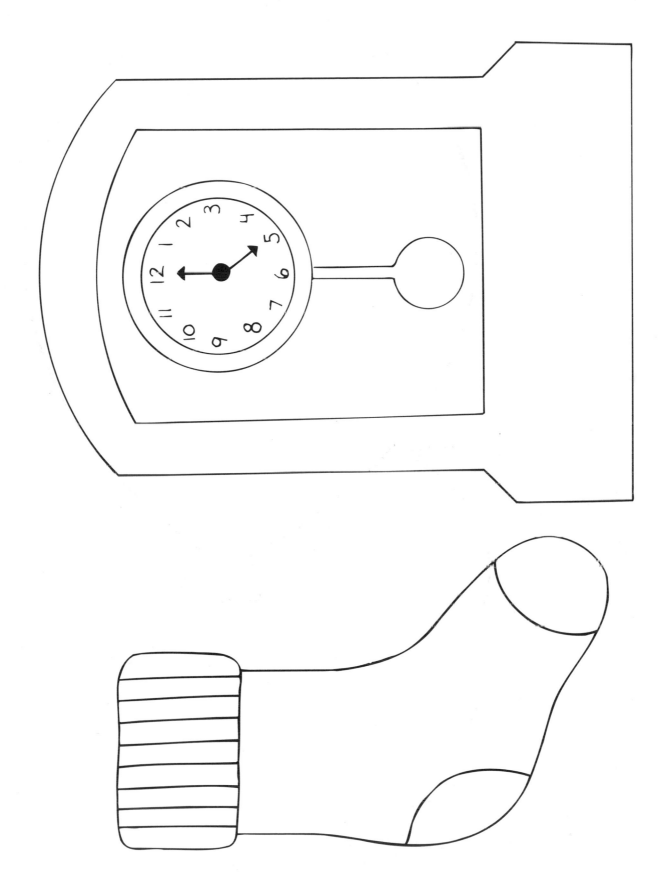

How Do Dinosaurs Say Good Night?

Written by Jane Yolen • Illustrated by Mark Teague
Blue Sky Press, 2000

● ● ● ● ●

A variety of dinosaurs and their human parents are preparing for bedtime. First the Papas come into each dinosaur's bedroom to find him or her stomping, pouting, throwing teddy bears about and requesting "One book more!" Then the Mamas take a turn with a very sweet and calm ending. This is the perfect storytime book with its simple, humorous, rhyming text and absolutely beautiful illustrations!

Activity: Glove Puppet Fingerplay

Using the pattern below, make a set of five felt dinosaurs to use with the following fingerplay.

Sleepy Dinosaurs

Sung to the tune: "Row, Row, Row Your Boat"

5 (4,3,2,1) yawning dinosaurs
Nod their sleepy heads.
One picks up his teddy bear
And shuffles off to bed.
(Remove one dinosaur.)

Take Home: Yawning Dinosaur

Materials Needed

- photocopies of yawning dinosaur from page 61
- tagboard
- clothespins
- crayons
- double-stick tape
- pinking shears

Prior to your storytime, photocopy and cut out a dinosaur (and its jaw) for each child. (Cut the dotted lines on the dinosaur's mouth and jaw with pinking shears to form the dinosaur's teeth. See the illustration on page 61.) Have the children color a dinosaur and jaw. Assemble the pieces onto the clothespin for them. The dinosaur should be attached with double-stick tape to the top portion of the clothespin near the pinked teeth. Attach the jaw to the lower part of the clothespin in the same fashion, making sure the end of the jaw is slipped behind the dinosaur. When the clothespin is pinched the dinosaur will open its mouth in a yawn!

pattern pieces

front view

back view

Is There Room on the Feather Bed?

Written by Libba Moore Gray • Illustrated by Nadine Bernard Westcott
Orchard House, 1997

This is a story about a wee fat man and his wee fat wife who live in a tiny house they share with a variety of animals. All get along very well except for a little skunk who keeps his distance at the request of the other animals. One day, a big storm blows in and floods the nearby brook just as the couple is going to bed. The storm is so bad that the animals come knocking two at a time at the couple's door, requesting shelter from the storm. Each request from the animal pairs is greeted by the little woman's reply, "Why bless your hearts, such a noise, such a fuss. There's room on the feather bed for all of us." This continues throughout the night until all but the little skunk are in the feather bed. That is, until it gets too bad outside for the little skunk, and he also comes knocking at the door.

Activity: Flannel Board Accompaniment

Use the patterns from pages 63–67 to make the characters from this delightful book. I know this seems like a lot of work for one program, but because of the variety of animals you will find endless uses for them. Examples that come to mind include "Old MacDonald," versions of "The Giant Turnip" and with the addition of a fox and gingerbread man, "The Gingerbread Man." I'm sure you can think of many more. This is one of those stories that delight children due to an absurd situation. Just as in "Ten Apples Up on Top," they love to see the additions of items grow to an unbelievable amount. Though the book easily stands alone, using the characters allows the children to become involved in the process. During the story the characters are added to the bed by you or the children, taking cues from the book. Encourage children to chant the little woman's repeated reply as the characters are added.

Take Home: Feather Bed

Materials Needed

- photocopies of the bed from page 67 and the characters from page 68
- glue sticks
- children's scissors
- crayons

Prior to your storytime, photocopy the characters and the bed, making sure you have one set per child attending. (Do not enlarge the bed for this activity.) Depending on the age of your group you may want to precut the characters. Have the children color the bed, then glue the characters onto it.

Adjust to desired size.

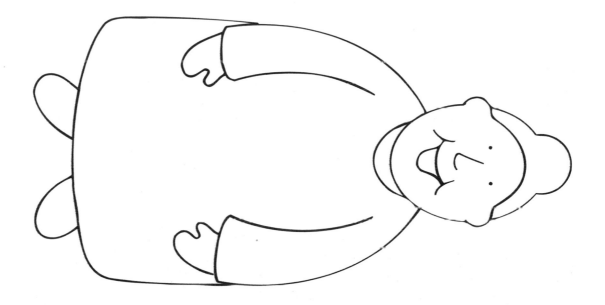

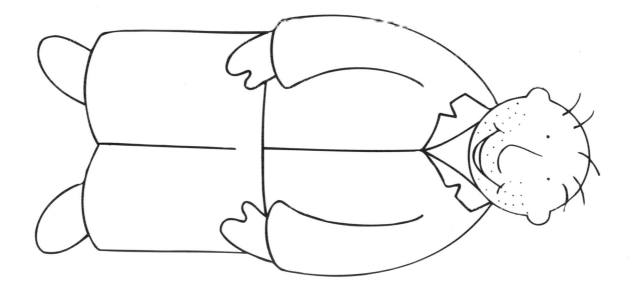

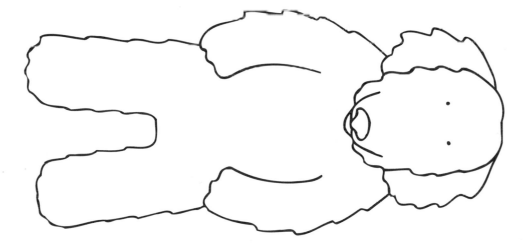

For the flannel board, enlarge to desired size
to accommodate all of the characters.

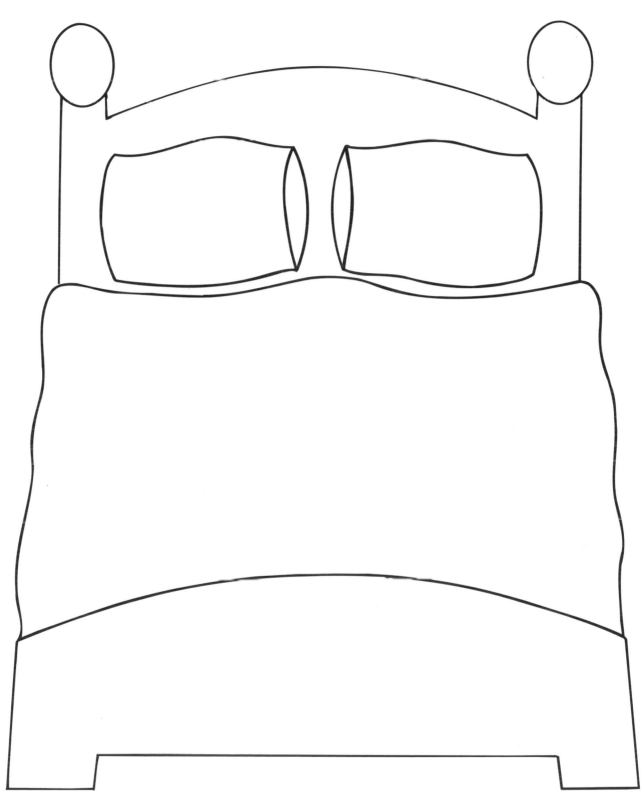

Joseph Had a Little Overcoat

Written and illustrated by Simms Taback
Caldecott Medal Winner, 2000 • Viking, 2000

Simms Taback adapted this wonderful book from a Yiddish folk song about a man named Joseph whose overcoat becomes old and worn from much use. Joseph recycles the coat into a jacket. When the jacket becomes worn he makes a vest from it and so on through numerous items of clothing until he is left with a button, which he loses. This doesn't stop Joseph though; he proceeds to write a book about his overcoat and its transformations, proving that "you can always make something from nothing." Adding to the beautiful illustrations are the die-cut holes that give clues to what Joseph will make next. As an extra bonus, the music for the folk song is included.

Activity: Flannel Board Accompaniment

Joseph Had a Little Overcoat is a fun book to share with groups. This activity, which accompanies the book, is intended to echo the transformations of Joseph's coat seen through the die-cuts, but also increase the size of the visual for larger groups.

Use the patterns from pages 70–72 to make the articles of clothing and the book from felt. Remember that all of the items (except the book) originated from one overcoat, so use the same color of felt for all of them. In preparation for storytime, stack the items on your flannel board following the sequence in the story. (The patterns are scaled so that each item will completely cover the item beneath it in sequence. Keep this in mind if you enlarge the patterns.) As you read, remove the top item to reveal the one underneath after it has been disclosed in the book. Near the conclusion of the story, all of the items on your flannel board will have been removed. (Place the felt book on the flannel board when clued by the text.)

Take Home: Overcoats

Materials Needed

- photocopies of overcoats from page 73
- crayons
- buttons
- Tacky glue

Prior to your storytime, photocopy and cut out one overcoat per child. Let the children color the overcoats. When they finish, assist them in folding the overcoats on the dotted lines so that they will open and close like true coats. Let each child pick a button from your button supply and glue it to the inside of the coat with tacky glue. From overcoat to button!

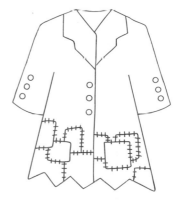

Adjust to desired size.

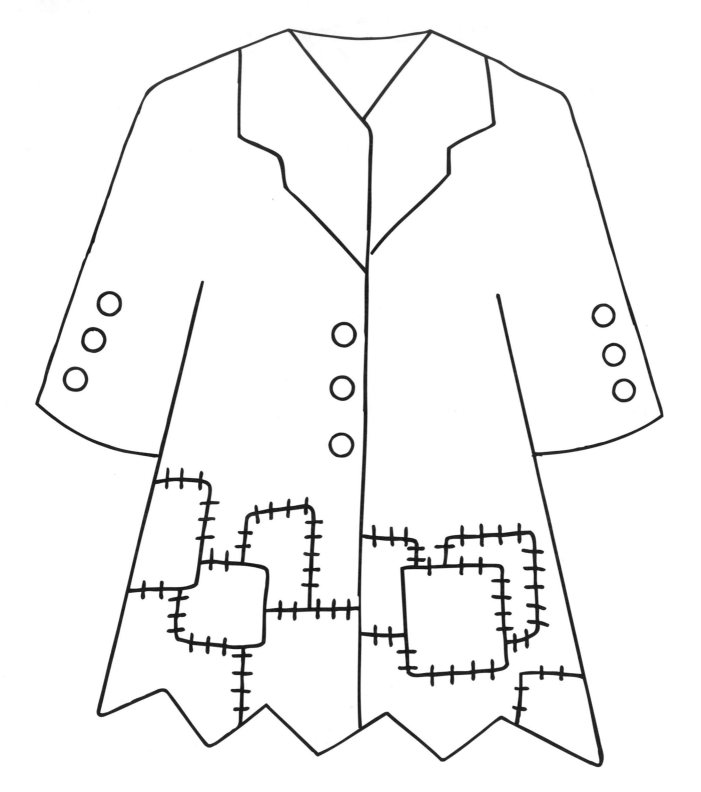

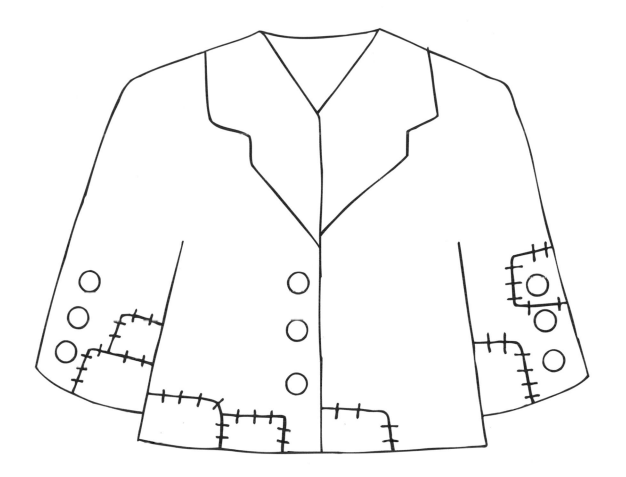

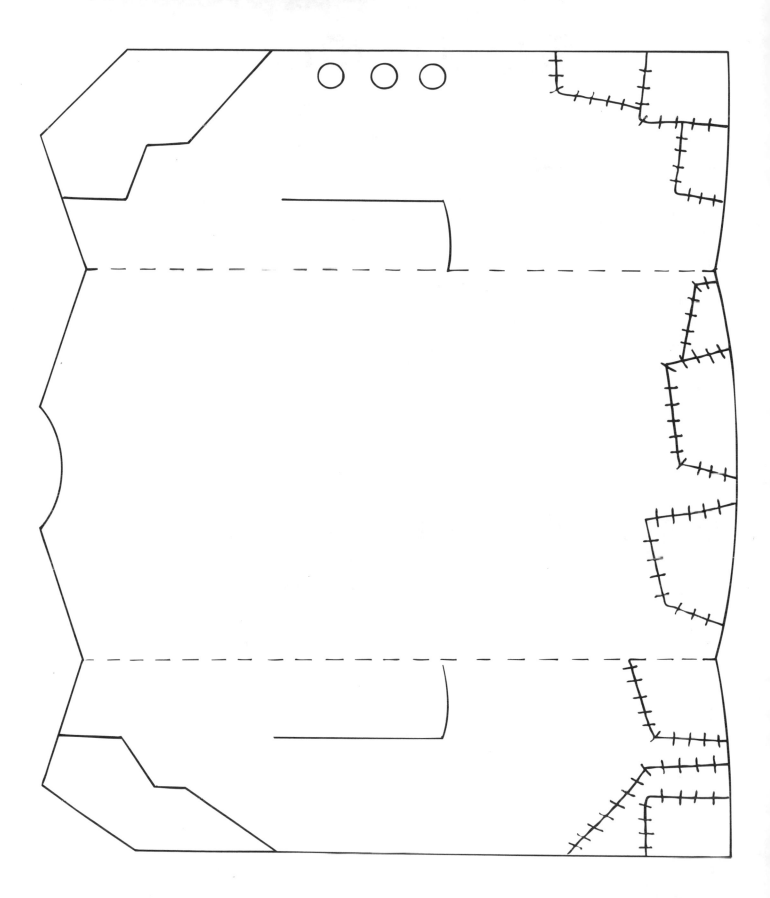

Lilly's Purple Plastic Purse

Written and illustrated by Kevin Henkes
Greenwillow Books, 1996

Lilly, in her signature red cowboy boots, is off to school and she loves everything about it! Lilly looks forward to going to school every day, but one Monday she is especially excited. Over the weekend she went shopping with her Grammy and returned with a new pair of movie star sunglasses, three shiny quarters and a purple plastic purse, all of which she intends to show to everyone at school. But trouble brews when Mr. Slinger asks Lilly to wait until an appropriate time to share her treasures with the class. When Lilly can't contain her excitement any longer and disrupts the class, Mr. Slinger takes her things to keep in his desk until the end of the day. After recovering from the initial shock of losing her treasures, her temper flares and she draws a not-so-nice picture of Mr. Slinger, which she leaves in his book bag. After school her things are returned to her and on her way home she finds a note inside her purse from Mr. Slinger promising a better day tomorrow. Oh no! What about the horrible picture she drew? How can she fix this mess she has gotten herself into?

Activity: Flannel Board Song

Use the patterns from pages 76–77 to make the boot, glasses, coins and purse in the appropriate colors of felt. (You may want to add gemstones or glitter to the sunglasses.) After sharing *Lilly's Purple Plastic Purse* with your group, lead them in singing the following song.

Lilly Has a Purple Purse

Sung to the tune: "Mary Had A Little Lamb"

Lilly has a purple purse,
(*Place purse on flannel board.*)
Purple purse, purple purse.
Lilly has a purple purse,
A purple plastic purse.

Lilly has three shiny quarters,
(*Place coins on flannel board.*)
Shiny quarters, shiny quarters.
Lilly has three shiny quarters,
Three shiny, jingly quarters.

Lilly has brand-new sunglasses,
(Place sunglasses on flannel board.)
New sunglasses, new sunglasses.
Lilly has brand-new sunglasses,
New movie star sunglasses.

Lilly wears red cowboy boots,
(Place boots on flannel board.)
Cowboy boots, cowboy boots.
Lilly wears red cowboy boots,
Red cowboy boots with stars.

Take Home: Lilly's Purse

Materials Needed

- photocopies of purse on tagboard from page 78
- purple crayons or markers
- tape

Prior to your storytime, photocopy the purse onto tagboard and cut out one purse per child. (The purse handle is formed by cutting on the bold curved line and folding on the dotted line, forming a flap for the top of the purse.) Have the children color a purse. Fold on the dotted lines, noting which side to fold down so as not to have the children's artwork end up on the inside of the purse! Tape the sides closed before folding the flap down. (As shown below.)

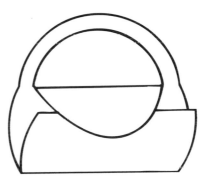

Fold as shown.

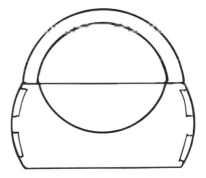

Adjust to desired size.

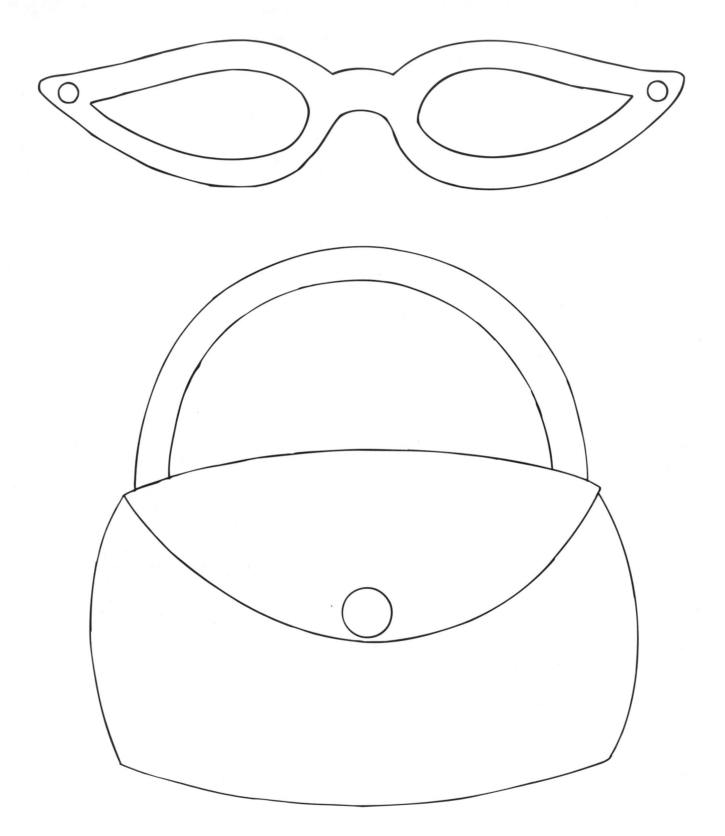

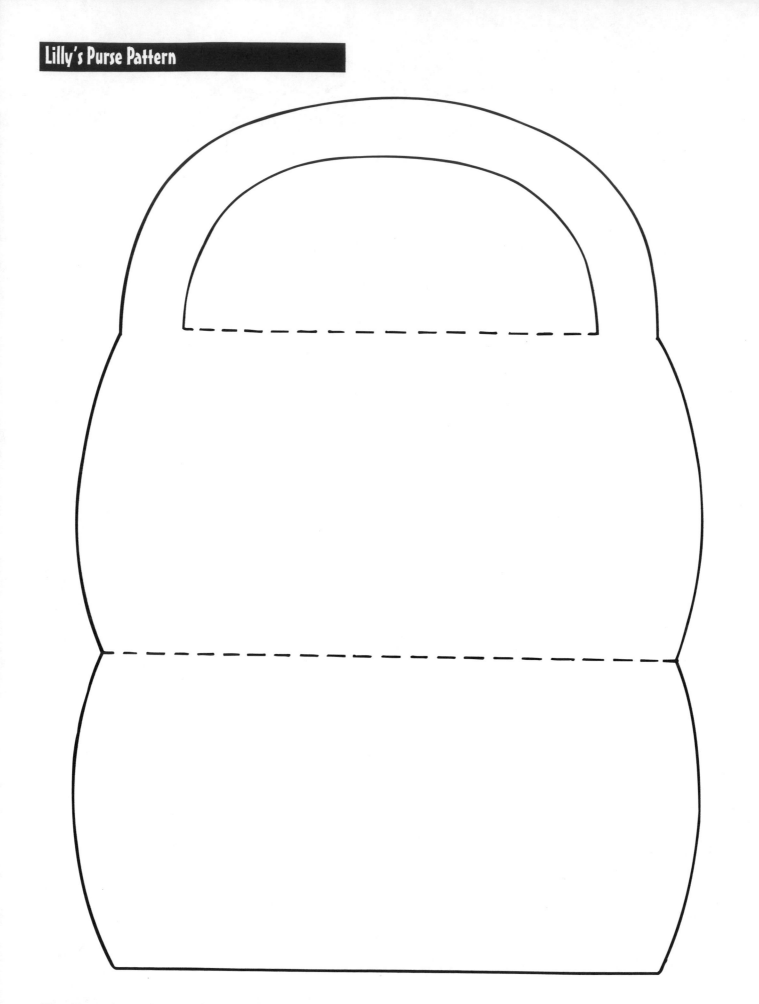

The Magic Hat

Written by Mem Fox • Illustrated by Tricia Tusa
Harcourt, 2002

A magic hat blows into town one day and every person the hat lands on turns into an animal of one sort or another. A wizard appears just as mysteriously to put everything right again, then leaves, taking the magic hat with him. The illustrations are beautiful! With a catchy, rhyming text and surprises with every turn of a page, this book is great fun at storytime!

Activity: Glove Puppet Fingerplay

Use the patterns from page 80 to make a set of hats from felt. You may choose to make five of the same hats or five different hats. After you have the basic hats, decorate them with extra touches such as flowers, polka dots, etc. When you are finished, add Velcro to the back of each to use on a puppet glove. After sharing *The Magic Hat,* lead the children in the following rhyme.

Five Magic Hats

5 (4, 3, 2, 1) magic hats, 5 (4, 3, 2, 1) magic hats,
They move like this, they move like that.
(Move hand side to side.)
One spun through the air, turning upside down,
(Remove one hat.)
Sat on a head, then blew out of town!
(Hold hat on your head, then whisk it away.)

Take Home: Finger Puppet

Materials Needed

* photocopies of puppet from below
* crayons

Prior to your storytime, photocopy and cut out one puppet per child. (The curved solid line in the middle should also be cut.) Have the children color their puppet. Demonstrate how to fold it on the dotted lines, form the hat and place it on their finger.

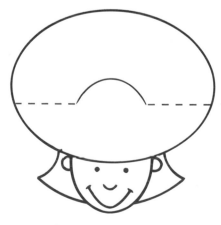

finger puppet pattern

Max

Written and illustrated by Bob Graham
Candlewick Press, 2000

● — ● — ● — ● — ●

Max is not like other little boys his age. He lives in the only house in the neighborhood shaped like a lightning bolt. His parents are the famous superheroes Madam Thunderbolt and Captain Lightning. His grandparents, who live with him, are retired superheroes. Even his dog Phantom wears a mask! The only thing about Max that is like other children is that he can't fly, which is very disturbing to his family. Even the kids at his school don't understand why he isn't more like his mom and dad. But Max shows no interest in flying, not until a baby bird falls from its nest outside Max's window. After flying to rescue the bird, Max finds it nearly impossible to stay grounded. Will Max follow in his parent's footsteps and become a legendary superhero also? "Not important," says Madam Thunderbolt. "Let's call him a small hero, a small hero doing quiet deeds. The world needs more of those."

Activity: Fingerplay

Use the patterns from pages 82–83 to make the superhero and five baby birds from felt. As in the story, the birds in this fingerplay are falling from a tree, so if you have a tree glove it would be perfect to use. The superhero puppet is not difficult to make. First assemble the entire front of the puppet. Then glue on the back of the shirt using glue only on the edges and none on the bottom. This will form a pocket for your fingers. After the back of the shirt is on, glue the cape into place as indicated on the pattern. The puppet will be worn on the hand opposite the birds. You can make him "fly in for the rescue" by slipping your fingers into the back of his shirt, under the cape. The birds will need Velcro on the backs to hold them on the glove. Now you're ready to share the book and the fingerplay with your group!

Five Baby Birds

5 (4, 3, 2, 1) baby birds,
Falling from a tree.
Crying, "Cheep, cheep, cheep, cheep,
Please help me!"
In flies our superhero,
His cape flapping in the breeze.
He catches one baby bird,
And brings him down safely!

Take Home: Superhero Kites

Materials Needed

- photocopies of superhero from page 84
- red material
- tape
- yarn
- crayons

Prior to your storytime, photocopy and cut out one superhero for each child. Also cut red material into capes, one for each superhero, using the pattern from page 83 as a guide. Let the children color their superheroes, then assist them with attaching the cape and yarn to the back.

Baby Bird Puppet Pattern

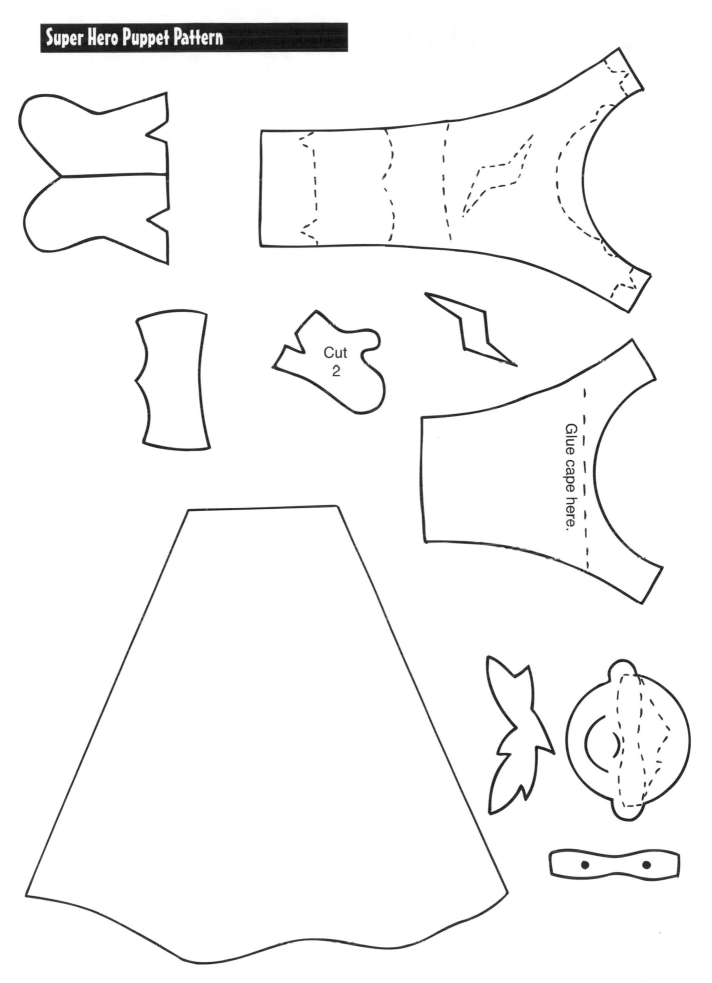

Cut
2

Glue cape here.

Mouse Paint

Written and illustrated by Ellen Stoll Walsh
Harcourt, 1989

Three white mice find three jars of paint—red, yellow and blue. They think it's mouse paint and each one jumps into a jar. After stepping into the puddles each has made, they discover three new colors. When they finish exploring with the colors they take a bath in the cat's water dish. (This always gets a laugh from the children.) As these adorable mice learn to mix new colors the children get a lesson, too! Amazingly simple text, wonderful illustrations and fun, fun, fun!

Activity: Flannel Board Song

This book lends itself to many activities reinforcing its subject matter. I have presented it many times using mice made from felt and jars of food coloring. While it's loads of fun, it can be very messy. This activity isn't messy, but it does involve making lots of mice—six whole mice and three halves, to be exact. Begin by making three mice from white felt using the pattern from page 87. Next, using the same pattern, make three more, one from red felt, one blue and one yellow. Now make three halves (using the pattern, cut off below the tail) one each from orange, purple and green felt—and glue these onto "puddles" of felt paint as shown in the illustration on page 87. When presenting the second verse of the following rhyme, place the half mice directly over the bottom half of the corresponding whole, colored mice. (Refer to the illustrated guide on page 88 to get the correct color mixes!) If you didn't know how to mix colors before, you will now!

After sharing *Mouse Paint* with your group, lead them in the following song.

Three White Mice

Sung to the tune: "Three Blind Mice"

Three white mice,
(Place mice on flannel board.)
Three white mice.
Three jars of paint,
Three jars of paint.
One jumps in the yellow,
(Swap one white mouse for the yellow one.)
One jumps in the red,
(Swap another white mouse for the red one.)
One jumps in the blue,
Up over his head.
(Swap last white mouse for the blue one.)
The mice that were white,
Are now painted instead.
No white mice.

Three painted mice,
Three painted mice.
Three puddles of paint,
Three puddles of paint.
The yellow's in red,
(Place orange half in red puddle over yellow's feet.)
And the red is in blue.
(Place purple half in blue puddle over red's feet.)
The blue's in the yellow,
(Place green half in yellow puddle over blue.)
They mix through and through.
Now there are six colors,
Three are brand new.
No white mice!

Take Home: Color Mice

Materials Needed

- plastic colored Easter eggs (red, yellow and blue)
- pipe cleaners (purple, orange and green)
- wiggle eyes
- felt scraps (for ears)
- Tacky glue

For this craft you will need enough plastic Easter eggs to be able to mix and match tops and bottoms of the eggs to end up with the same color combinations as the mice in the book but with a twist. The pipe cleaner (that will be used for the tail) will act as the result of the combination of two colors being mixed together. For example, a red top, a blue bottom and a purple pipe cleaner tail. (Red mixed with blue makes purple.) Ears should be cut from red, blue and yellow felt and matched with the tops of the eggs. To attach the tails, make a small hole in the center of the bottom of the egg (it is easiest to do this before your storytime). Have the children thread the pipe cleaner though the hole and secure with glue on the inside.

Note: You may want to put together little packets of "mouse parts" prior to your storytime to hand out to the children. You will have three different color combination packets—red top, blue bottom, purple tail; blue top, yellow bottom, green tail; yellow top, red bottom, orange tail. Each packet should include one egg top with two felt ears of the same color, one egg bottom, one pipe cleaner and one set of wiggle eyes.

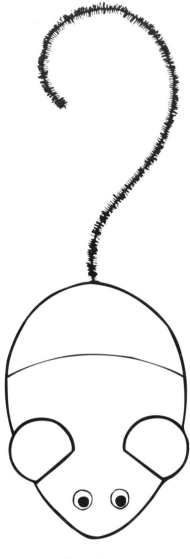

sample craft

Adjust to desired size.

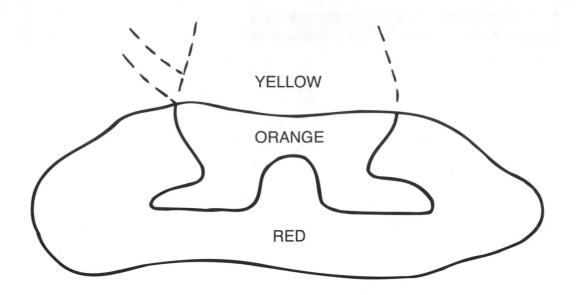

YELLOW

ORANGE

RED

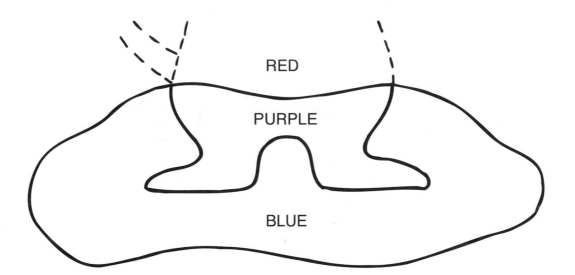

RED

PURPLE

BLUE

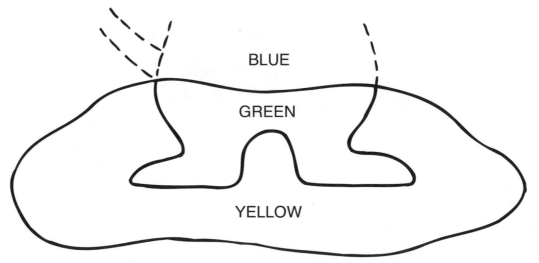

BLUE

GREEN

YELLOW

My Crayons Talk

Written by Patricia Hubbard • Illustrated by G. Brian Karas
Henry Holt & Company, 1996

● ● ● ● ●

How would a crayon describe its color if it could talk? A little girl with a very talkative box of crayons lets each one do just that. With the repeating phrase, "Talk, talk. My crayons talk. Yackity, clackity. Talk, talk, talk." Not only do these crayons talk, they also sing, yell, scream and shout. Red roars, gold brags and blue calls: "Sky, swing so high!" The illustrations are delightful and, of course, very colorful!

Activity: Fingerplay Song/Glove Puppets

Use the pattern at right to make five crayons from felt—one each from red, blue, yellow, green and orange. (You can also use colors of your choice, then make the appropriate changes in the rhyme.) Attach Velcro to the back of each crayon to use on a puppet glove. After sharing *My Crayons Talk*, lead the children in the following song using the suggested colors and items or your own.

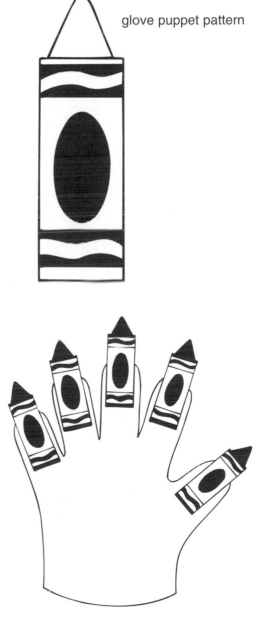

glove puppet pattern

Talking Crayons

Sung to the tune: "Row, Row, Row Your Boat"

My crayons talk to me.
They tell me which to use.
If I wanted to color the sky,
Which one would I choose?
(Wait for the children to respond and then remove the blue crayon.)

Additional Verses:

Grass/green
Bananas/yellow
Apples/red
Oranges/orange

89

Take Home: Crayon Paper Bag Puppet

Materials Needed

- photocopies of puppet from pages 91–92
- lunch-size paper bags
- crayons
- tape or glue sticks

In preparation for your storytime, photocopy and cut out a set of puppet parts for each child. Have the children color the puppets and then attach them to the paper bags using tape or glue sticks. If preferred, the puppets can be photocopied onto construction paper and then assembled, eliminating the need for coloring.

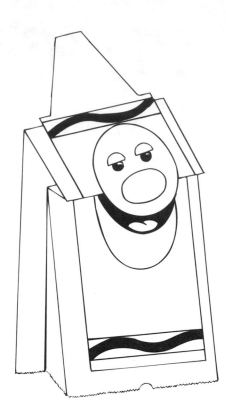

top piece

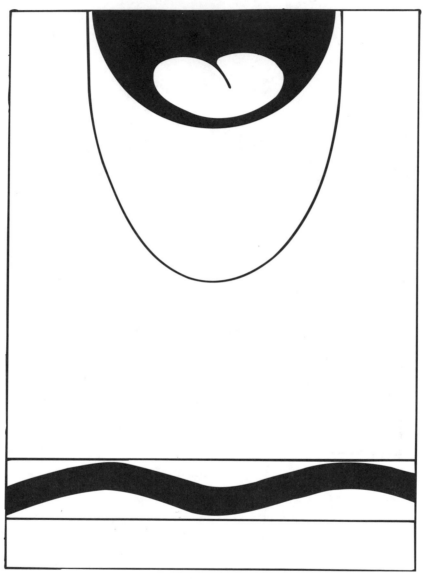

bottom piece

The Paperboy

Written and illustrated by Dav Pilkey • Caldecott Honor Book, 1997
Orchard Books, 1996

—————— • —————— • —————— • —————— • ——————

This book is about a morning in the life of a paperboy and his dog. The young boy and his dog wake up to prepare for the delivery of the newspapers even though everyone else in the family is still sleeping. They quietly walk down the stairs to the kitchen for breakfast, go to the garage to fold the papers and then head out on the route. "All the world is asleep except for the paperboy and his dog. And this is the time when they are the happiest." With the route finished and the sun rising, the boy with his empty bags and his dog head for home. When they arrive, they find the family slowly waking and they crawl back into bed, their job complete. This is one of the sweetest stories I have ever read! It makes you love and admire this little boy and his faithful dog. The illustrations are delightful and large, making it a perfect book for sharing.

Activity: Fingerplay on Glove

Use the illustration as a guide to make five newspapers from white felt. To begin, cut rectangles approximately 3 ½" x 2" and use a fine-tipped permanent maker to make the top portion of each rectangle resemble the front page of a newspaper. Next roll the felt from the bottom so the headline shows. Secure with hot glue. Add Velcro to the back of each newspaper. After sharing *The Paperboy* with your group, lead them in the following fingerplay.

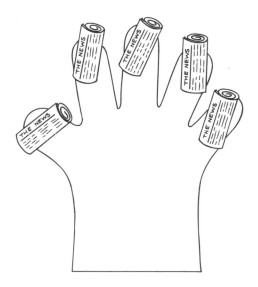

glove puppet pattern

Paperboy

Sung to the tune: "This Old Man"

5 (4, 3, 2, 1) newspapers in a sack,
Strapped onto the paperboy's back.
The paperboy delivers one,
Then he peddles on.
The paperboy's job will soon be done.

Closing Verse:
1 newspaper in a sack,
Strapped onto the paperboy's back.
The paperboy delivers one,
Then he peddles on.
Now the paperboy's job is done!

Take Home: Newspaper Hats

Materials Needed

- old newspapers
- markers
- stickers
- tape

Prior to your storytime, collect enough newspapers to make one hat for each child. The hats can be made ahead of time for large groups, but if you are working with a small group, or have help, the children will enjoy watching the process of a sheet of newspaper becoming a hat. The hats require one rectangular section of newspaper of at least double thickness. Follow the illustrations below to fold your hats. When the hats are completed, have the children decorate them with crayons, markers or stickers.

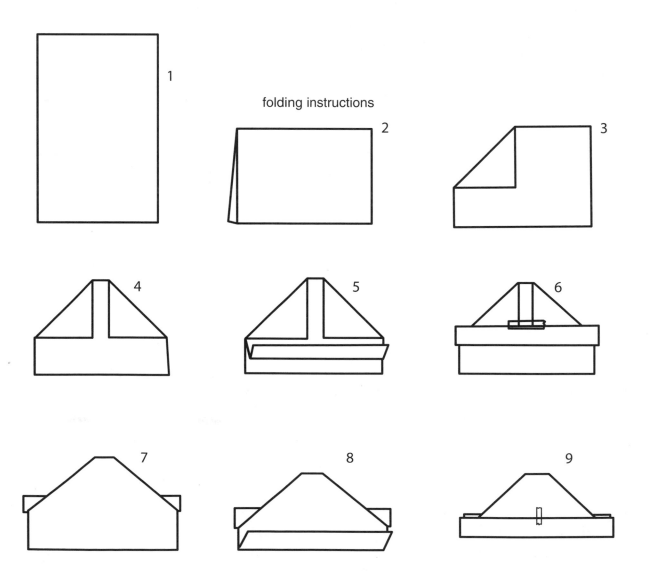

folding instructions

Sheep on a Ship

Written by Nancy Shaw • Illustrated by Margot Apple
Houghton Mifflin, 1989

Pirate sheep set sail on a sea trip and run into stormy weather. They find themselves facing wind, rain and hail, and although they give it their best, they are forced to abandon ship. They board a raft and finally reach land only to fall short when attempting to jump from their raft to the dock! "Sheep climb out. Sheep drip. Sheep are glad to end their trip." A delightful rhyming text and wonderful illustrations make this a fun book to share during storytime.

Activity: Flannel Board Fingerplay Song

Use the patterns from pages 96–97 to make five pirate sheep from felt. To give each sheep a little more character, add boots to one, a sword to another and so on. As in the illustration, you may also wish to make their ship, which would add a fun visual to enhance the rhyme. (To make the ship, increase the size on the copier if you need a pattern.) After sharing *Sheep on a Ship* proceed with the following song.

Five Pirate Sheep

Sung to the tune: "Five Green and Speckled Frogs"

5 (4, 3, 2, 1) pirate sheep set sail,
They get wet from head to tail,
In a storm with lots of rain and hail.
They grab their pails to bail.
One gets too close to the rail!
Uh oh, oh no! Overboard he fell!
(Remove one sheep.)

Take Home: Pirate Hats

Materials Needed

- tagboard
- photocopies of pirate hats from page 98
- crayons
- tape

Prior to your storytime, photocopy onto tagboard and cut out one hat per child. (Cut all bold lines including the center.) Cut strips of tagboard approximately 12" long and 3" wide to use when fitting the hats to the children. Have children color the hats and fold on the dotted lines. Assist the children by attaching the strip to the inside center front of the hat, then have them put the hat on as you determine how long to leave the strip, then secure it with tape to the inside of the back of the hat.

95

Adjust to desired size.

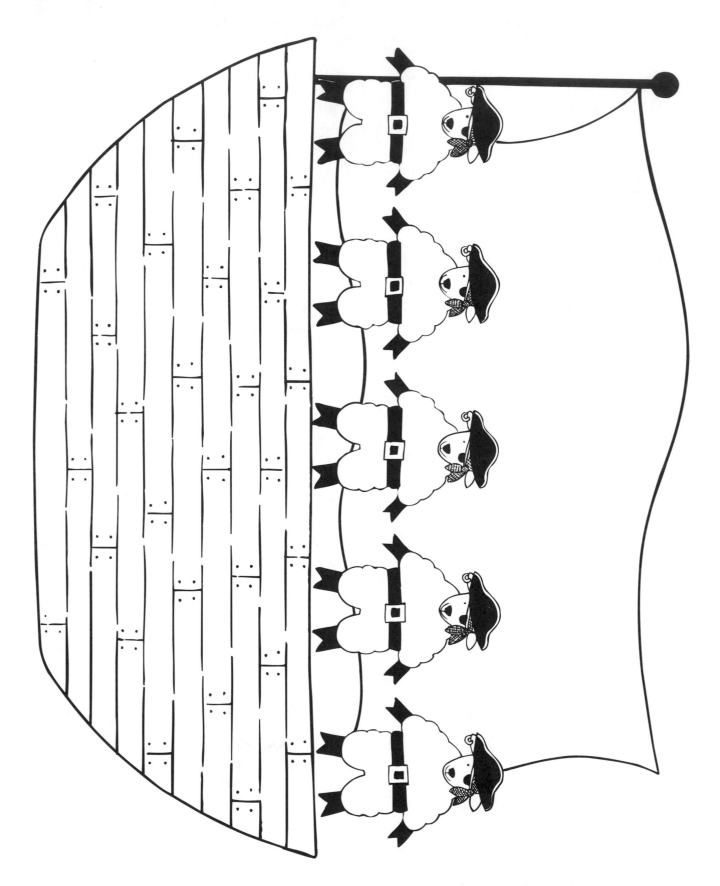

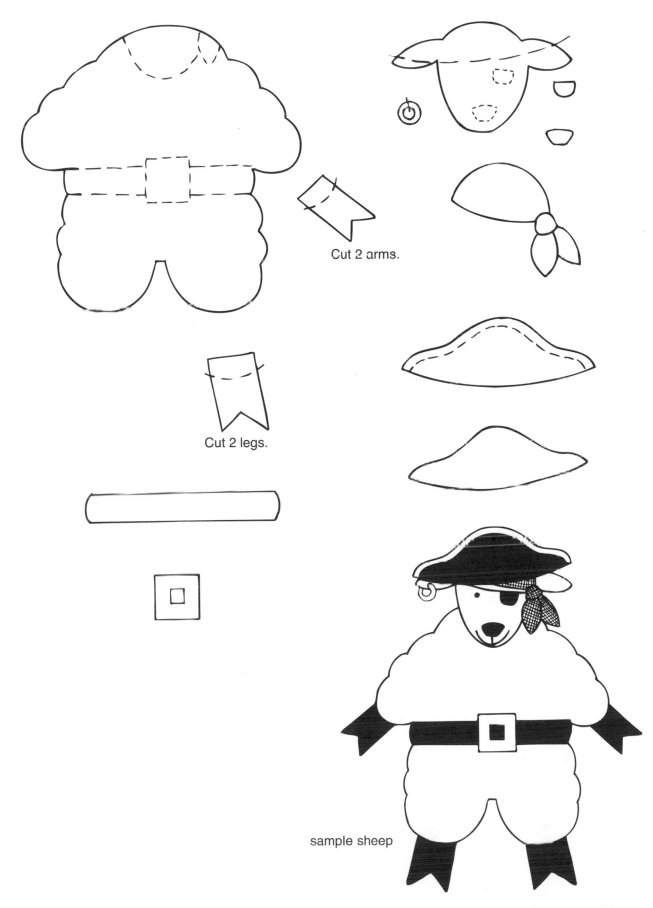

Cut 2 arms.

Cut 2 legs.

sample sheep

Pirate Hat Pattern

Enlarge to desired size.

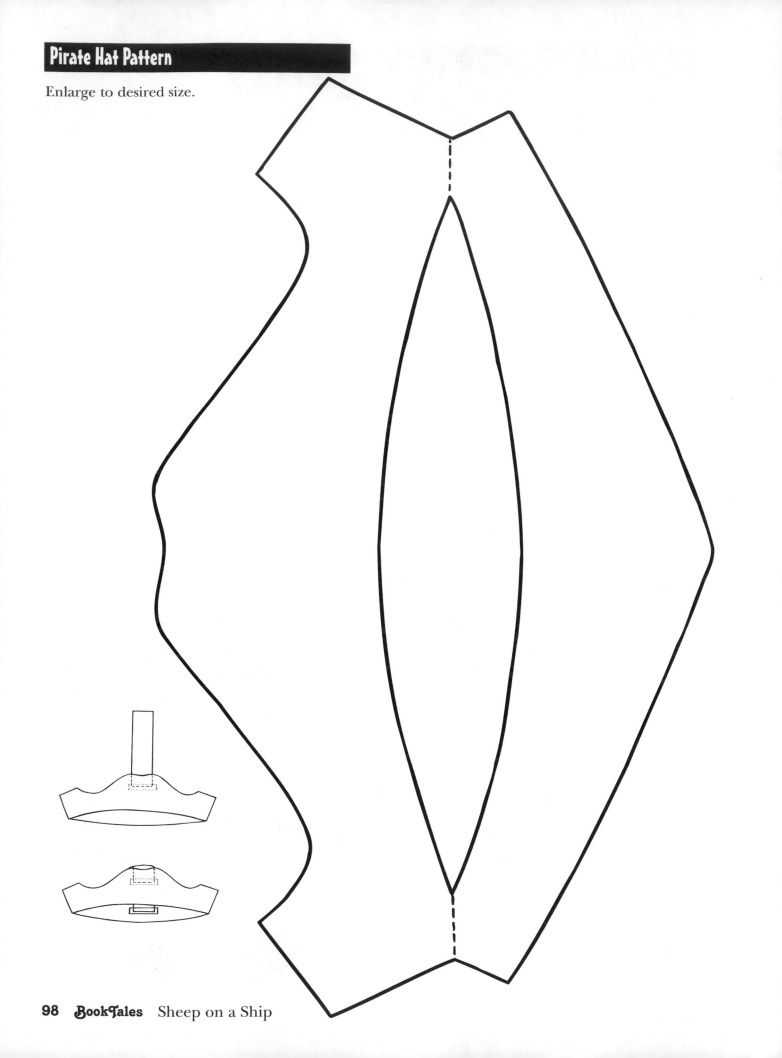

Silly Sally

Written and illustrated by Audrey Wood
Harcourt Brace, 1992

In this rhyming story a character named Silly Sally travels to town walking backwards and upside down. Along the way, she meets several animals with whom she engages in different activities. She dances a jig with a pig, plays leapfrog with a dog, sings a tune with a loon and falls asleep with a sheep. While they all sleep, another character named Neddy Buttercup appears. He wakes them up one by one and they all finish the trip together.

Activity: Flannel Board Song

Use the patterns from pages 101–108 to make Sally and her friends for your flannel board. Because the characters need to be turned upside down, use stiffened felt if possible. This will make manipulating the characters much easier during your presentation. Refer to the characters in the book to choose felt colors. Complete the character's details with a fine-tipped permanent maker. After sharing *Silly Sally*, present the following rhyme.

Sally Went to Town

Sung to the tune: "The Farmer in the Dell"

Sally went to town, *(Place Sally on flannel board.)*
Sally went to town.
She went to town, she's upside down,
(Flip Sally upside down.)
Sally went to town.

She met a silly pig, *(Add pig.)*
She met a silly pig.
She met a pig, they danced a jig,
(Flip pig upside down.)
She met a silly pig.

She met a silly dog, *(Add dog.)*
She met a silly dog.
She met a dog, they played leapfrog,
(Flip dog upside down.)
She met a silly dog.

She met a silly loon, *(Add loon.)*
She met a silly loon.
She met a loon, they sang a tune,
(Flip loon upside down.)
She met a silly loon.

She met a silly sheep, *(Add sheep.)*
She met a silly sheep.
She met a sheep, they fell asleep,
(Flip sheep upside down.)
She met a silly sheep.

Neddy woke them up, *(Add Neddy.)*
Neddy woke them up.
He woke them up, he's right side up,
Neddy woke them up.

They all went to town,
They all went to town.
They went to town, all upside down,
(Flip Neddy upside down.)
They all went to town.

Take Home: Silly Sally Puppet

Materials Needed

- photocopies of puppet at right
- crayons
- tape
- craft sticks or straws

Prior to your storytime, photocopy and cut out one puppet per child as needed. Have the children color their puppets. Assist them with folding on the solid line and taping to the craft stick or straw. Demonstrate to the children how their Silly Sally puppet can walk forwards, backwards or upside down!

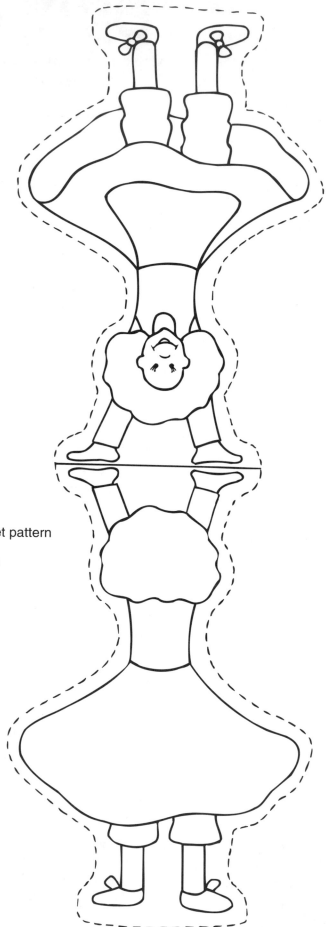

puppet pattern

Adjust to desired size.

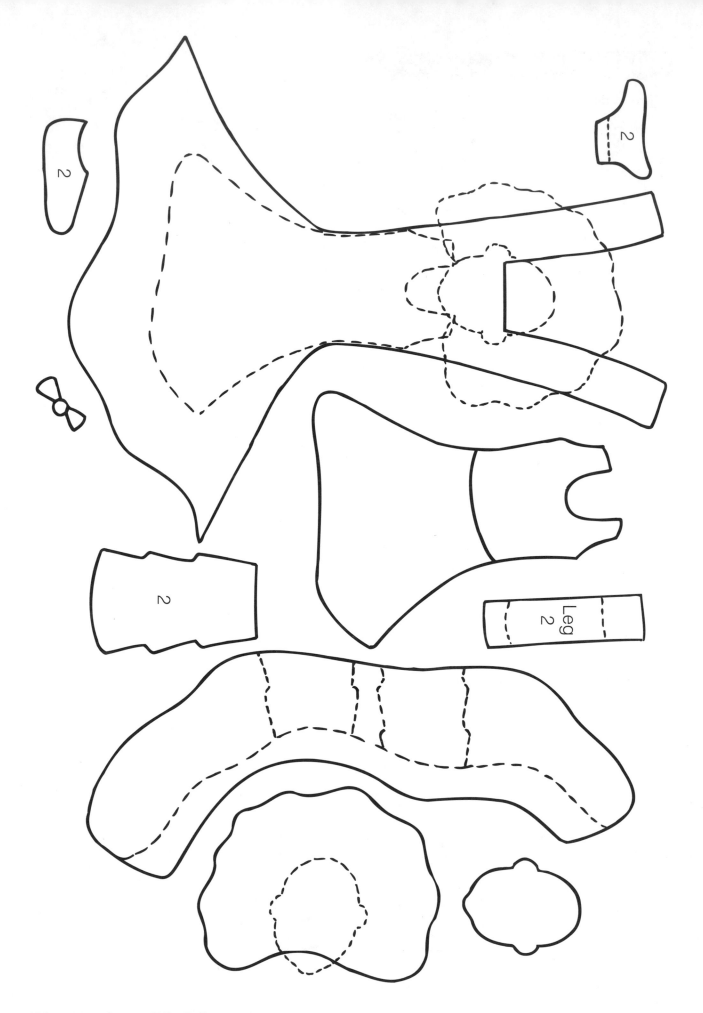

Leg
2

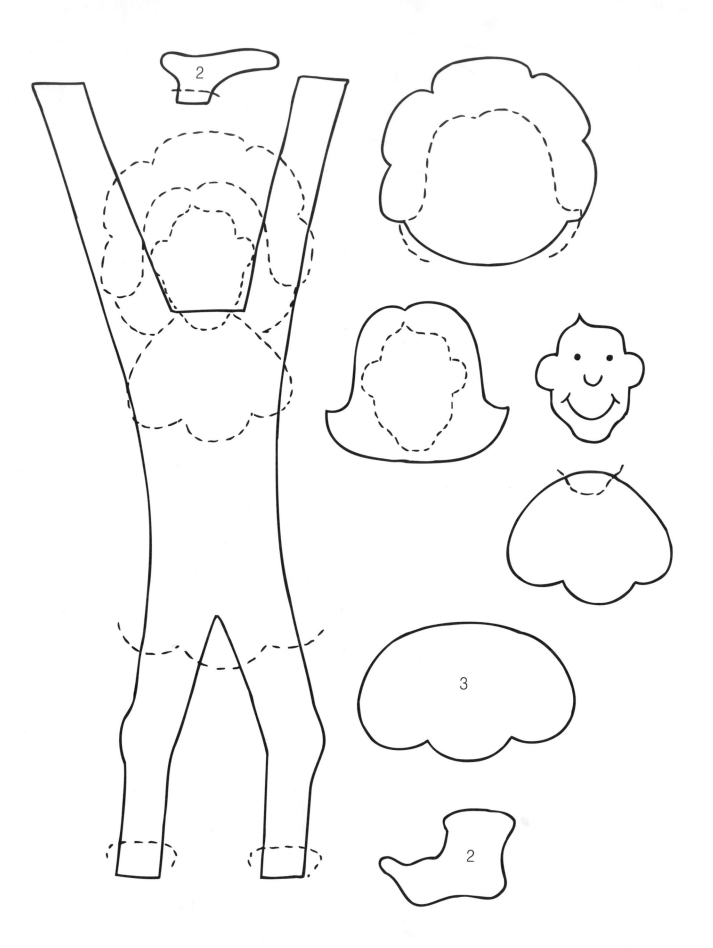

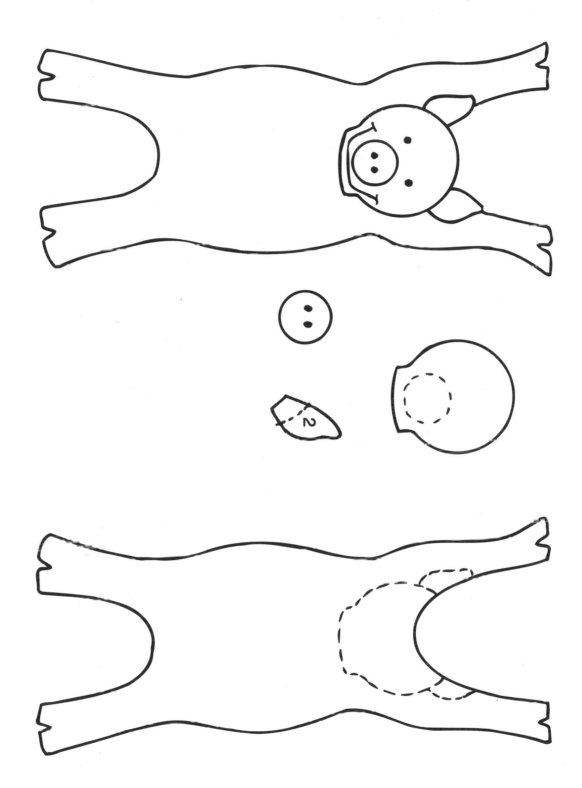

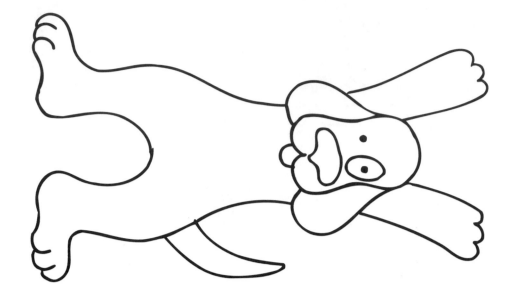

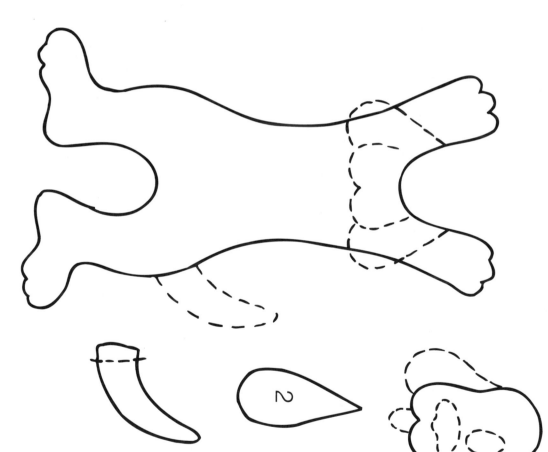

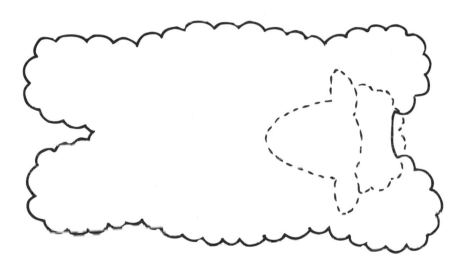

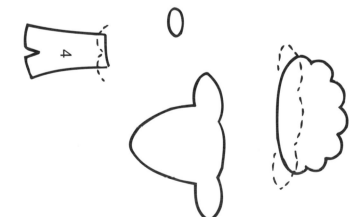

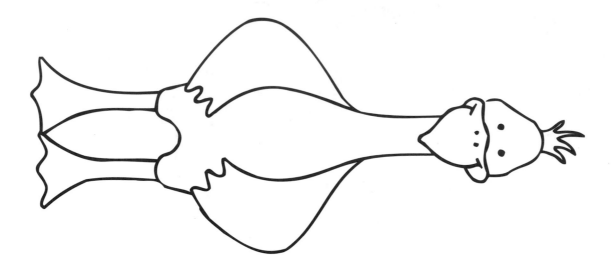

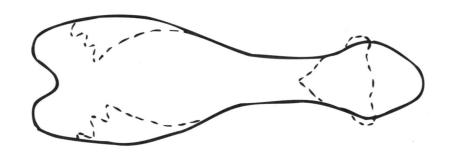

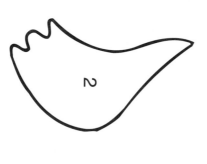

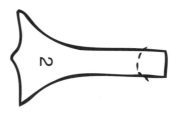

Six Hogs on a Scooter

Written by Eileen Spinelli • Illustrated by Scott Nash
Orchard Books, 2000

The Hog family has transportation trouble on their night out to the opera. When the family car won't start they try taking a scooter. When the tires on the scooter go flat they try roller skates and so on, until a city bus finally delivers them to the opera house but, sadly, too late. The opera is over and worse yet, there are no more buses until morning! After discussing their options they decide to spend the night at the bus stop and catch the first bus home in the morning. "Six hogs sleeping at a bus stop makes a very interesting sight!" This repeating phrase with humorous text and illustrations makes this a fun book to share.

Activity: Flannel Board Rhyme

Use the patterns from pages 110 to make six hogs and the scooter in an appropriate size for your flannel board. (Set up the characters on your flannel board as shown below.) After sharing the book with your group, lead the children in the following rhyme.

Six Silly Hogs

Sung to the tune: "Are You Sleeping"

Six silly hogs
On a scooter,
What a sight!
An interesting sight!
One thinks he just might
Jump off, what a sight!
There he goes! *(Remove one hog.)*
There he goes!

Take Home: "What a Sight Hog Spectacles"

Materials Needed

- photocopies of spectacles from page 111 (on tagboard)
- crayons

Extend the arms of the glasses to reach over the children's ears. Make enough copies for each child to have a pair. Precut the glasses, making sure to cut out the lenses following the dotted lines on the pattern. Let the children color their glasses, then help them fold the arms at the point indicated on the pattern.

Flannel Board Patterns

Adjust to desired size.

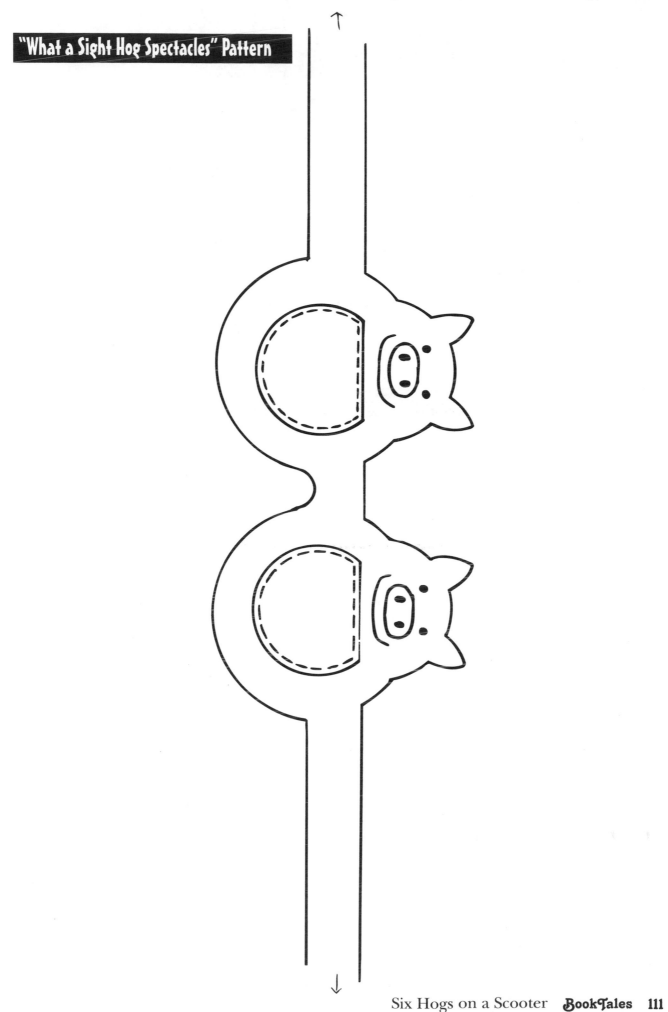

Snowballs

Written and illustrated by Lois Ehlert
Harcourt Brace, 1995

Large, beautiful collages illustrate this story about building a family of snowmen with objects saved in a paper bag. They start with a snow dad and continue to include the whole family and their pet dog and cat. "Guess you know what happened when the sun came out." One by one the family melts and nothing remains but a snowball. Children love to point out the objects used on the snowmen—the toy tires for the snow boy's ears, the forks for the baby's arms, etc. At the end of the story the author includes pictures of the items she used and photographs of real snowmen.

Activity: Flannel Board Song

Use the patterns from pages 114–115 to make the snow family and pets from felt. (The snowmen's accessories can be made from bright colors of felt to add a little interest to all the white.) You will need to enlarge all the patterns to make the characters more suitable to use with large groups of children. After sharing *Snowballs* with your group, lead them in the following rhyme.

Snow Family

Sung to the tune: "The Farmer in the Dell"

We're building a snow dad,
(Place snow dad on flannel board.)
We're building a snow dad.
He's made of snow from head to toe,
We're building a snow dad.

We're building a snow mom, *(Add snow mom.)*
We're building a snow mom.
She's made of snow from head to toe,
We're building a snow mom.

We're building a snow boy, *(Add snow boy.)*
We're building a snow boy.
He's made of snow from head to toe,
We're building a snow boy.

We're building a snow girl, *(Add snow girl.)*
We're building a snow girl.
She's made of snow from head to toe,
We're building a snow girl.

We're building a snow baby, *(Add snow baby.)*
We're building a snow baby.
She's made of snow from head to toe,
We're building a snow baby.

We're building a snow dog, *(Add snow dog.)*
We're building a snow dog.
He's made of snow from head to toe,
We're building a snow dog.

We're building a snow cat, *(Add snow cat.)*
We're building a snow cat.
She's made of snow from head to toe,
We're building a snow cat.

Our snow family is now done,
Our snow family is now done.
They're made of snow from head to toe,
Our snow family is now done!

Take Home: Coffee Filter Snowballs

Materials Needed

- coffee filters
- hot glue sticks
- white tissue paper
- tape

Prior to your storytime, hot glue two coffee filters together around the edge leaving an opening large enough for the children to stuff (about 3 inches). Prepare enough filters for each child to have one. Supply the children with a prepared coffee filter and about two sheets of tissue paper. Have the children tear the tissue into small pieces and stuff them into the filter. When they have completed stuffing the coffee filter, assist them in taping it closed at the opening.

Adjust to desired size.

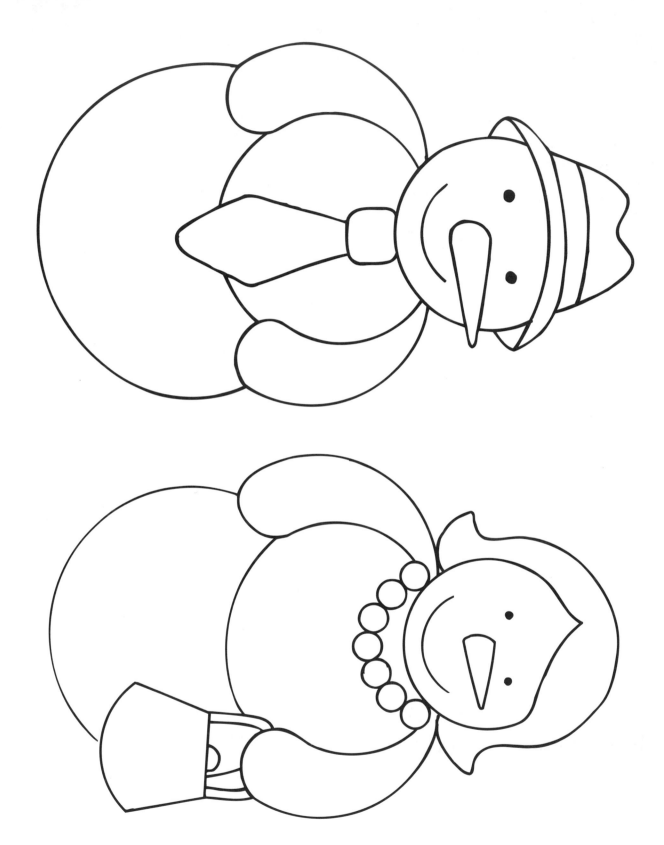

The Stray Dog

Written and illustrated by Marc Simont • From a true story by Reiko Sassa
Caldecott Honor Book, 2002 • HarperCollins, 2001

A family goes on a picnic in a park and meets a stray dog who spends the day with them. When it is time to go home they leave the dog they call Willy behind but think about him all the next week. They return to the park the following Saturday hoping to see Willy. They do see him, but only briefly as he is being chased by the dogcatcher. The family convinces the dogcatcher that Willy is theirs by producing a collar and a leash, which are actually the brother's belt and the sister's hair ribbon. This time Willy leaves with the family when the picnic is over!

Activity: Fingerplay

Use the pattern from page 118 to make five dogs in a variety of felt colors. This pattern is sized for use on a glove board as described in the introduction, so you may want to shrink it if you intend to use the dogs on a glove. After sharing *The Stray Dog* with the children, reinforce the story with the following fingerplay.

Five Stray Dogs

5 (4, 3, 2, 1) stray dogs,
Wishing for a home,
Sitting in the park,
Feeling all alone.

Along comes a family,
To the park one day.
They play with one dog,
And they take him home to stay!
(Remove one dog.)

Take Home: Dog Finger Puppet

Materials Needed

- photocopies of dog puppet pattern at right
- tagboard
- crayons
- tape

Prior to your storytime, photocopy onto tagboard and cut out enough dog puppets for each child to have one. Have the children color their puppets. Assist them with folding and taping the puppet at the nose and on the bottom. Be sure to leave the back of the ear open for their finger. Demonstrate to the children that by wearing the puppet on your middle finger you can make the dog's legs with your other fingers and thumb as shown in the illustration below.

puppet pattern

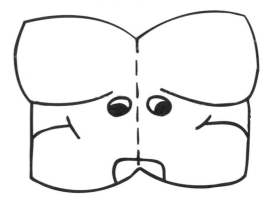

Flannel Board Patterns

Adjust to desired size.

Ear 2

sample dog

Ten Apples Up On Top

Written by Theodore LeSieg • Illustrated by Roy McKie
Random House, 1961

A lion balancing first one, then two apples on his head is challenged by a dog who thinks he can do more. As the two continue with the competition, increasing the level of skill by hopping and climbing trees without dropping the apples, they are challenged by a tiger who claims he can outdo them both. As the number of apples increases, the rivalry between the three turns into a team effort to keep the apples on top of their heads. They finally reach their goal of ten apples and are beaming with pride over their accomplishment when they are confronted by a bear, armed with a broom, and the chase is on!

Activity: Flannel Board Accompaniment

Use the patterns from pages 120–121 to make a lion from yellow felt with an orange felt mane. You will also need to make ten red apples from felt. Adjust the size of the patterns to suit your needs—the bigger the character and apples are, the more dramatic the visual will be! In preparation for storytime, check to see if your flannel board needs to be positioned vertically so that there is room for all ten apples to fit on top of the lion's head. When introducing the book, discuss with the children the difficulty, as well as the silliness, of balancing apples on your head. (Demonstrate if you're feeling silly.) While sharing the book with the children place the apples on the lion's head when cued by the story. Take your cue from the apples, not the characters, when adding apples—the children love watching the tower grow! As the apples increase, build the excitement with comments about the children's achievements and encourage their comments also. The second half of the book will be smooth sailing. After ten, there will be no more apples to add, just the excitement and anticipation of the outcome.

Take Home: "Ten Apples Up On Top" Headbands

__Materials Needed__

- strips of tagboard for headbands
- precut apples
- glue sticks
- tape

In preparation, cut strips of tagboard suitable for headbands and enough apples from red construction paper for each child to have ten. (The pattern for the flannel board apple will work fine if you need one.) Have the children count out ten apples for themselves (assisting if needed) and glue them to their headband. When they have finished, size the headband to fit their head and tape in place.

Adjust to desired size.

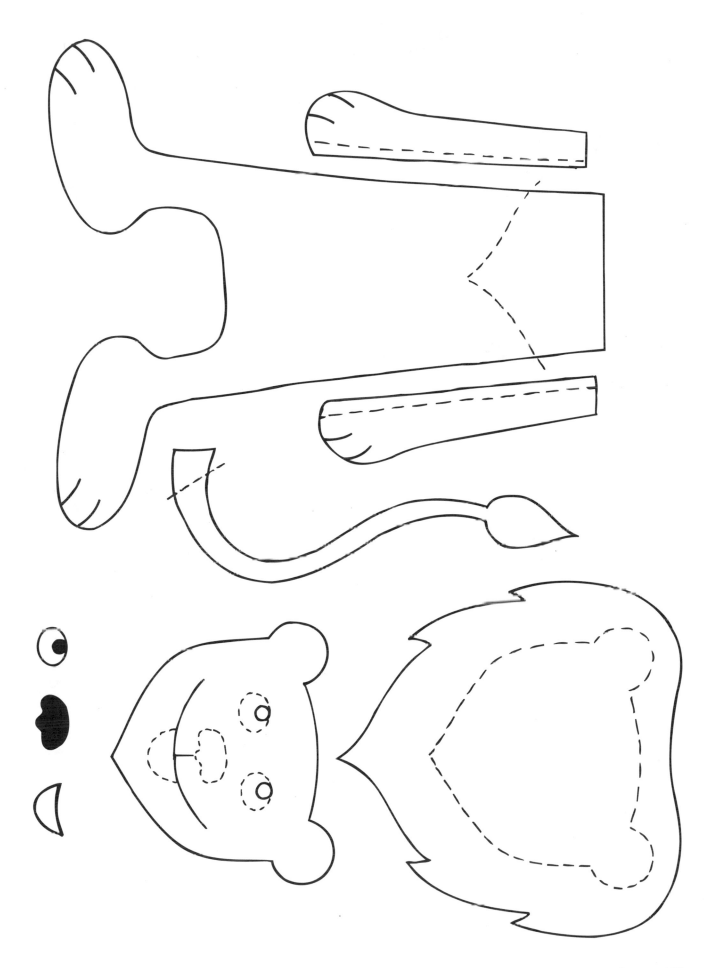

Trashy Town

Written by Andrea Zimmerman and David Clemesha
Illustrated by Dan Yaccarino • HarperCollins, 1999

Mr. Gilly, the trash collector, drives his trash truck to different locations all over Trashy Town to empty the trash cans. The text has a wonderful rhythm that adults as well as children love to repeat. "Dump it in, smash it down, drive around the trashy town." The reader gets to follow along with Mr. Gilly as he gives a tour of all the trash locations in town. At each stop he asks the same question: "Is the trash truck full yet?" The children love to answer with an enthusiastic: "NO!" Mr. Gilly continues on his rounds until there is only one more thing in town to clean up—Mr. Gilly himself!

Activity: Fingerplay Song

Use the pattern at right to make a set of five garbage cans from gray felt. (Stiffened felt works well for this project.) Since the cans and the lids are separate you may want to make "trash" from scraps of felt and then glue the lids on top and at an angle as shown in the illustration. When complete, add Velcro to the backs. After sharing *Trashy Town* with the group, lead them in the following fingerplay.

The Garbage Truck

Sung to the tune: "Pop Goes the Weasel"

All around the trashy town,
5 (4, 3, 2, 1) cans sit filled to the brim.
The garbage truck comes rumbling by,
One gets dumped in! *(Remove one can.)*

Closing Verse:
All around the cleaned-up town,
The streets are all trash free.
Always use the garbage cans,
And our town won't be trashy!

garbage can pattern

Take Home: Mr. Gilly Treat Cup

Materials Needed

• photocopies of man and garbage can cover from page 123

• small bathroom paper cups (3 oz.)

• crayons

• tape

Prior to your storytime, photocopy and cut out both items. Have the children color their pieces. Assist them with wrapping the cup with the can cover, then attaching the man.

sample treat cup

The Treasure

Written and illustrated by Uri Shulevitz • Caldecott Honor Book, 1980
Farrar, Straus and Giroux, 1978

A poor man named Isaac has a dream in which a voice tells him to go to the Royal Palace in the capital city and search for a treasure under the bridge. When he wakes up he decides to pay it no attention, but after having the same dream on two other nights, Isaac sets off on a journey to the capital city. It is not an easy trip, as he has to walk through forests and over mountains to reach his destination. When he finally arrives he is hesitant to search for the treasure because he finds the bridge is guarded day and night. He spends his time wandering around the area until the captain of the guard asks, "Why are you here?" When Isaac tells him about the dream the captain laughs at him and tells Isaac about a dream of his which leads Isaac to the surprise location of the treasure. This beautifully illustrated book has amazingly simple text that even very young children will enjoy.

Activity: Action Rhyme/Song

After sharing *The Treasure* with the children, lead them in the following action song.

Treasure Hunt

Sung to the tune: "The Farmer in the Dell"

On a treasure hunt we'll go, *(March in place.)*
A treasure hunt we'll go.
We're going on a treasure hunt,
On a treasure hunt we'll go!

We'll dig a hole that's deep, *(Digging motion.)*
We'll dig a hole that's deep.
We're going on a treasure hunt,
We'll dig a hole that's deep!

We'll pull the treasure out,
(Pulling motion, hand over hand.)
We'll pull the treasure out.
We're going on a treasure hunt,
We'll pull the treasure out!

We'll drag the treasure home,
(Dragging motion, marching in place.)
We'll drag the treasure home.
We're going on a treasure hunt,
We'll drag the treasure home!

Take Home: Treasure Chest

Materials Needed

- photocopies of treasure chest from page 125
- crayons
- tape
- "Treasure Treats"

Prior to your storytime, photocopy and cut out one treasure chest per child. Have the children color their treasure chest. When they have finished coloring, demonstrate and assist with folding the chests on the dotted lines and taping the sides closed, forming an envelope. As the children leave give each a treat, such as chocolate coins wrapped in gold foil, to put in their chests.

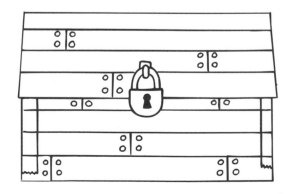

Treasure Chest Pattern

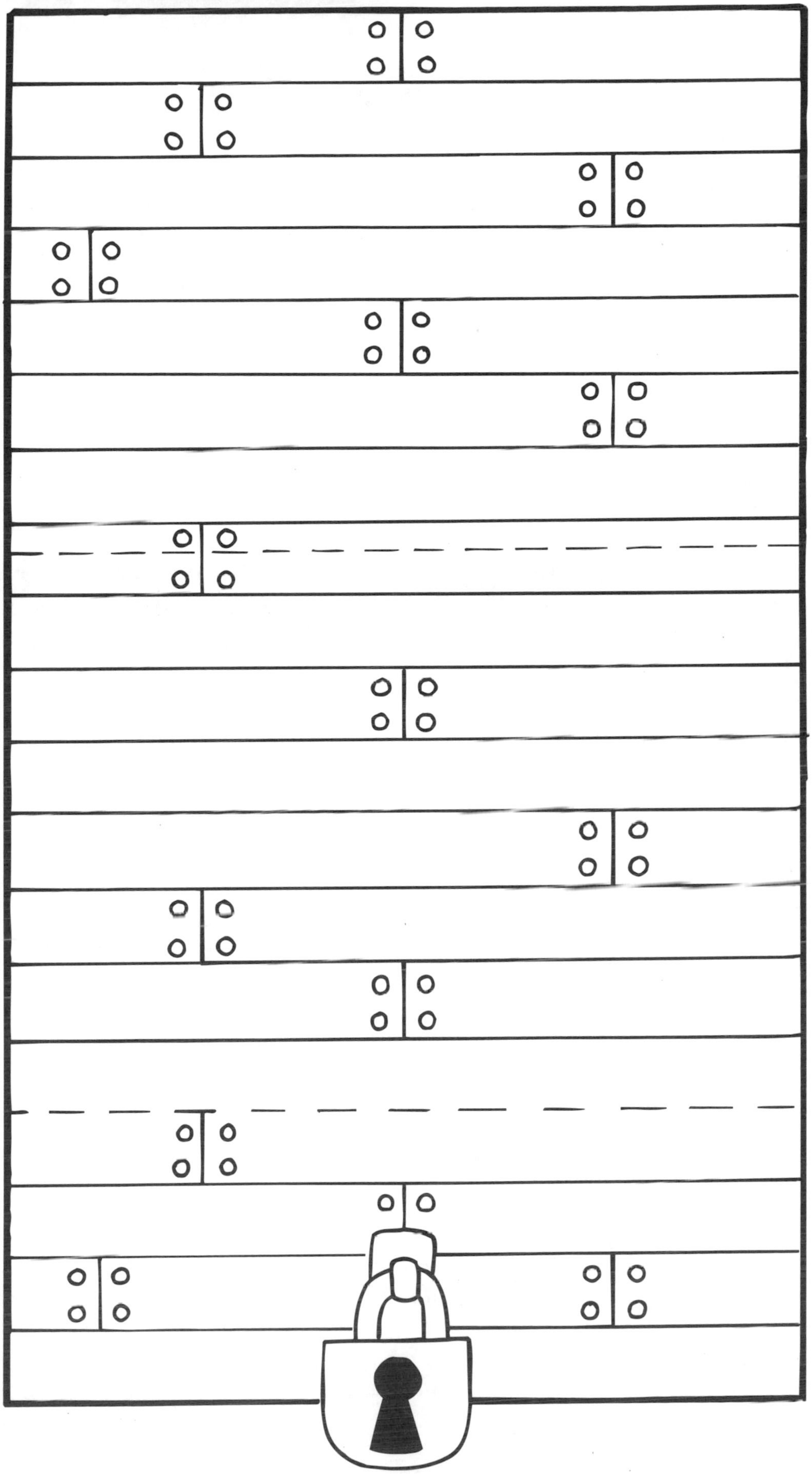

Where the Wild Things Are

Written and illustrated by Maurice Sendak
Caldecott Medal Book, 1964 • Harper, 1963

In this Caldecott award winner, a boy named Max, dressed in a wolf suit, causes so much mischief that his mother sends him to his room without his supper. While in his room, Max imagines a forest growing and his adventure begins. He sails to another land where Wild Things crown him king. After taming the Wild Things, Max becomes bored and decides to sail back home despite the pleas from his companions to stay. Arriving back in his room he finds his supper waiting.

Activity: Flannel Board Rhyme

Use the patterns from pages 127–128 to make five Wild Things from felt. You may also wish to fashion a simple tree limb from felt to go across the top of your flannel board for the Wild Things to swing from! (See illustration below.)

Wild Things

5 (4, 3, 2, 1) wild Wild Things,
Swinging from the trees.
One fell down
And skinned his knees.
He cried for Max
And Max said "Oh me!
That's what happens
When you swing from the trees!"

Take Home: Wild Thing Necklace

Materials Needed

- photocopies of Wild Thing from page 127
- crayons or markers
- tape
- yarn

Prior to your your storytime, photocopy and cut out a Wild Thing for each child. Have the children color their Wild Thing. Assist them in taping each end of a piece of yarn, long enough for a necklace, to each hand of the Wild Thing.

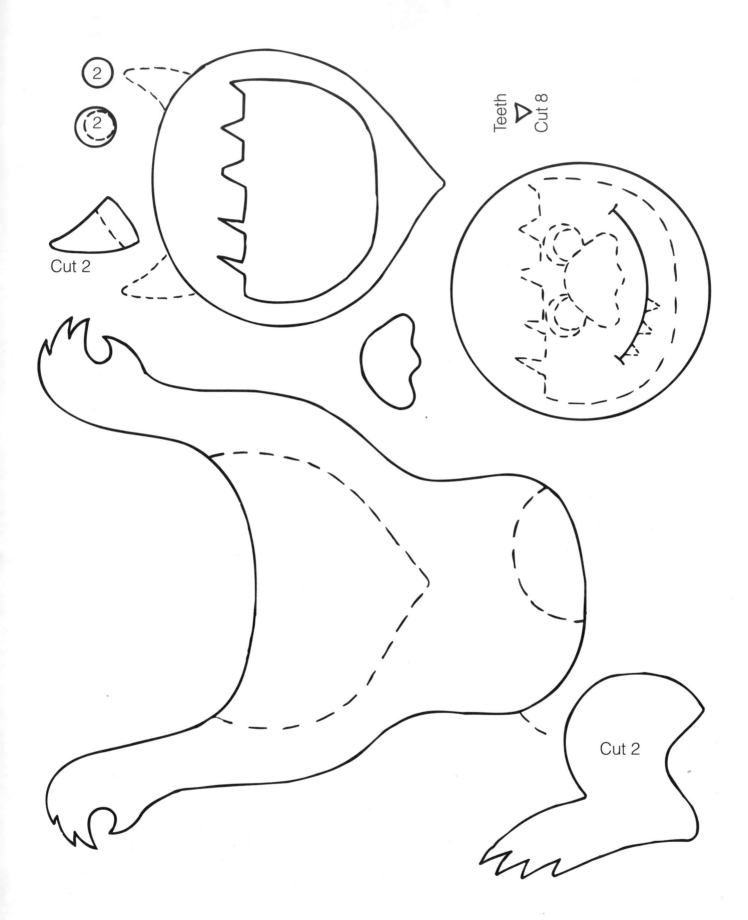

2

2

Cut 2

Teeth
Cut 8

Cut 2

Where the Wild Things Are